INTERPRETING BIBLICAL TEXTS

THE
PENTATEUCH

GENERAL EDITORS

Gene M. Tucker, *Old Testament*

———————————————

Charles B. Cousar, *New Testament*

INTERPRETING

I · B · T

BIBLICAL TEXTS

THE
PENTATEUCH

Terence E. Fretheim

ABINGDON PRESS
Nashville

THE PENTATEUCH

Copyright © 1996 by Abingdon Press

All rights reserved.

This book is printed on recycled, acid-free, elemental-chlorine-free paper.

Library of Congress Cataloging-in-Publication Data

Fretheim, Terence E.
　　The Pentateuch / Terence E. Fretheim.
　　　　p.　cm. — (Interpreting Biblical texts)
　　Includes bibliographical references and index.
　　ISBN 0-687-00842-5 (alk. paper)
　　　　1. Bible. O.T. Pentateuch—Criticism, interpretation, etc.
　　I. Title.　II. Series.
　　BS1225.2.F74　1996
　　222'.106—dc20　　　　　　　　　　　　　　　　　　　　96-33533
　　　　　　　　　　　　　　　　　　　　　　　　　　　　　　CIP

Scripture quotations, unless otherwise indicated, are from the New Revised Standard Version Bible, copyright © 1989, by the Division of Christian Education of the National Council of the Churches of Christ in the United States of America.

Scripture quotations noted RSV are from the Revised Standard Version of the Bible, copyright 1946, 1952, 1971 by the Division of Christian Education of the National Council of Churches of Christ in the USA. Used by permission.

98 99 00 01 02 03 04 05 — 10 9 8 7 6 5 4 3 2

MANUFACTURED IN THE UNITED STATES OF AMERICA

To my mother and father

from whom I first learned these stories

CONTENTS

PART TWO
THEMES AND STRATEGIES IN THE PENTATEUCH

FOREWORD

Biblical texts create worlds of meaning, and invite readers to enter them. When readers enter such textual worlds, which are often strange and complex, they are confronted with theological claims. With this in mind, the purpose of this series is to help serious readers in their experience of reading and interpreting, to provide guides for their journeys into textual worlds. The controlling perspective is expressed in the operative word of the title—*interpreting*. The primary focus of the series is not so much on the world *behind* the texts or out of which the texts have arisen (though these worlds are not irrelevant) as on the world *created by* the texts in their engagement with readers.

Each volume addresses two questions. First, What are the critical issues of interpretation that have emerged in the recent history of scholarship and to which serious readers of the texts need to be sensitive? Some of the concerns of scholars are interesting and significant but, frankly, peripheral to the interpretive task. Others are more central. How they are addressed influences decisions readers make in the process of interpretation. Thus the authors call attention to these basic issues and indicate their significance for interpretation.

Second, in struggling with particular passages or sections of material, how can readers be kept aware of the larger world created by the text as a whole? How can they both see the forest and examine individual trees? How can students encountering the story of David and Bathsheba in 2 Samuel 11 read it in light of its context in the larger story, the Deuteronomistic History that includes the books of Deuteronomy through 2 Kings? How can readers of Galatians fit what they learn into the theological

11

coherence and polarities of the larger perspective drawn from all the letters of Paul? Thus each volume provides an overview of the literature as a whole.

The aim of the series is clearly pedagogical. The authors offer their own understanding of the issues and texts, but are more concerned about guiding the reader than engaging in debates with other scholars. The series is meant to serve as a resource, alongside other resources such as commentaries and specialized studies, to aid students in the exciting and often risky venture of interpreting biblical texts.

Gene M. Tucker
General Editor, Old Testament

Charles B. Cousar
General Editor, New Testament

PREFACE

This volume is primarily concerned with introducing students to the Pentateuch in its canonical form. The long and complex history of its interpretation will influence what I say, of course, and in more ways than I realize. But my preeminent interest is to enable the student of the Pentateuch to come to know more fully the Pentateuch's basic content, not this theory or that.

I undertake this study out of an interest in the capacity of the Pentateuch to speak a word of/about God to modern readers. These texts speak a word *of* God in the sense that they are means by which God speaks words of judgment and grace to readers in every generation. Hence, I will be concerned about the rhetorical strategy of the Pentateuch, that is, those matters of style and content that are designed in such a way as to have a certain effect upon its readers. The most basic effect desired, I believe, is to shape the faith and life of the Pentateuch's readers. To use the language of Deut 6:2, "so that you and your children and your children's children may fear the LORD your God all the days of your life, and keep all his decrees and his commandments . . . so that your days may be long."

In the service of this desired effect, these texts also speak a word *about* God. To use the language of the foreword, they are designed to "create worlds of meaning, and invite readers to enter them. When readers enter such textual worlds . . . they are confronted with theological claims." This means that I will give special attention to the theology *in* the text, most particularly its claims about God.

To that end, two introductory chapters will introduce the reader to the study of the Pentateuch and will present a proposal for reading the Pentateuch in terms of its rhetorical strategy. The remaining five chapters will seek to discern how that strategy works itself out within each book of the Pentateuch, using somewhat different approaches in view of the nature of the texts.

Conversations with many individuals have helped prepare the way for this book. I wish to express my special appreciation to students in my Pentateuch classes at Luther Seminary for interacting with this material. I am grateful to the series editor, Gene Tucker, and to Beverly Stratton and Richard Nysse for reading portions of the manuscript and offering helpful suggestions for its improvement. I also wish to thank the administration and Board of Directors of Luther Seminary for granting me a leave of absence to complete this project.

OUTLINE OF THE PENTATEUCH

THE BOOK OF GENESIS

1:1–9:17	— Universal creation, fall, flood, promise
9:18–11:26	— Beginnings of world history
11:27–25:18	— Abraham, Sarah, and Hagar
25:19–36:43	— Isaac and Jacob, Rebekah and Rachel
37:1–50:26	— Judah, Joseph, and Jacob's family

THE BOOK OF EXODUS

1:1–15:21	— Sojourn in Egypt, Plagues, and the Exodus
15:22–18:27	— Wilderness Wanderings (I)
19:1–24:18	— Stay at Sinai; giving of law; covenant
25:1–31:18	— Tabernacle (I) and Priesthood
32:1–34:35	— Apostasy, forgiveness, and covenant renewal
35:1–40:38	— Tabernacle (II)

THE BOOK OF LEVITICUS

1:1–7:38	— Sacrifices and Offerings
8:1–10:20	— Ordination of Priests
11:1–15:33	— Issues of Purity

16:1-34   — The Day of Atonement

17:1–25:55   — Various ritual and moral matters

26:1–27:34   — Concluding exhortation and appendix

THE BOOK OF NUMBERS

1:1–10:10   — Census (I); Preparations for Departure from Sinai

10:11–25:18   — Wilderness Wanderings (II)

26:1–36:13   — Census (II); Preparations for Entrance into the land

THE BOOK OF DEUTERONOMY

1:1–4:43   — Retelling of the story from Sinai to Jordan

4:44–28:68   — Ten Commandments, with expansion and commentary

29:1–31:29   — Covenant with the new generation

32:1–33:29   — Song and Blessing of Moses

34:1-12   — Death of Moses

PART ONE

ISSUES IN READING THE PENTATEUCH

CHAPTER 1

THE STUDY OF
THE PENTATEUCH

PENTATEUCH, TORAH, AND LAW

The Pentateuch (that is, a book in five parts) has been a designation for the first five books of the Old Testament (and Hebrew Bible) since the second century CE at least. When it assumed this five-part form is not known. Though it may always have had such a form (the division is known to Philo and Josephus and probably earlier), the flow of the Sinai narrative from Exodus 19 *through Leviticus* to Numbers 10 suggests a later division. The five-part division may have been a formal move dictated by convenience in scroll handling (Exodus and Numbers are similar in length; Genesis and Deuteronomy are more independent in character). Yet, the shorter length of Leviticus, its particular content, and its place midpoint in the Pentateuch suggests that it was separated for religious purposes, reflecting the centrality of its concerns for the implied audience (see below).[1]

19

The biblical texts make no reference to this five-part form. They do refer to "(the book of) the law" (Ezra 10:3; Neh 8:3), but it is unclear whether this wording refers to the laws or to the entire Pentateuch (completed by 400 BCE or so). Moses is associated with "the law" from early in the postexilic era (2 Chron 23:18; 30:16), but its scope is again uncertain. The New Testament references to (the law of) Moses (cf. Luke 24:27, 44) assume this association (see Sir 24:23). Such references are likely a shorthand reference to the Pentateuch, as also in the phrase "the law and the prophets" (see Matt 5:17; Acts 13:15; Rom 3:21), and probably many other NT references to "the law" (e.g., Rom 7:1).

To the extent that these recurrent allusions to "the law" refer to the entire Pentateuch, they are misleading, whether they refer to its literary form or its most basic content. The basic form of the Pentateuch is not law, but narrative, moving from the creation to the eve of Israel's settlement in the promised land; laws have been woven into this narrative structure at various points. Moreover, the basic content of the Pentateuch is not legal in character; it is the story of God and (primarily) a people called Israel, often in interaction with each other. While a theological use of law, as revealing of Israel's sin, is present throughout the Pentateuch (see Deut 31:26), liberating words about God's gracious actions also punctuate the narrative. The Hebrew word *torah* can be more properly used if it is broadly defined as instruction, and hence could include both law and narrative. But, given the usual meanings of the word "law," it should not be used as a shorthand reference to the Pentateuch in its entirety.

THE PENTATEUCH AS BOOK OF FAITH

Interpreters through the centuries have found a home in the Pentateuch at several points. From the number of citations, Jesus and the New Testament authors seem especially attracted to Deuteronomy, perhaps because of its hortatory character. The preeminence of the law in early Judaism has long been noted. In more modern times, Genesis is the favorite, probably because of the creation texts and the family stories. This has been less true in scholarly circles, which have tended to lift up the book of Exodus, because of historical interests, a particular understanding of "salvation history," and a recognition of the constitutive character of the exodus and accompanying events for Israel as the people of God.

In the church, the Pentateuch has had more than a preparatory function for the Christian gospel; it has actually spoken an effective Word of God to ongoing communities of faith by calling, warning, exhorting, judging, redeeming, comforting, and forgiving. Because the church through the years has *experienced* the Pentateuch as Word of God in these ways, its liturgies, its preaching, and its catechetics have been filled with references to these texts.

Young Christians have been reared on the Pentateuch stories in particular, from the creation to Noah's ark with its parade of animals to the tower of Babel; from the near-sacrifice of Isaac to Jacob's wrestling to Joseph's coat of many colors; from the baby Moses set adrift on the Nile to Israelites walking through the sea on dry land to the gifts of water and manna in the wilderness. Catechisms that include the Ten Commandments have been impressed upon their memories and have given shape to their speech and action. Liturgies have had built into their very center the themes of Passover and unleavened bread, and Exodus 15 has been appointed as a text for Easter Sunday, so cosmic is the victory of God seen to be.

The New Testament discerns many continuities between the Pentateuch and the experience of the early church, with texts cited as warning (1 Cor 10:6-11), apologia (Acts 7:17-44), instruction (1 Cor 9:8-12; 10:11; 2 Cor 8:14-15), specifications of what love requires (Rom 13:8-10; Matt 19:16-22), paradigms of sin and failure (Rom 5:12-21; 1 Cor 15:21-22), examples of faith and faithfulness (Romans 4; Galatians 3; Hebrews 11), reminders of its missional purpose (1 Pet 2:9-10; Rev 1:5-6; 5:10), and resources for an eschatology (Rev 8:6–9:21; 15:1-5; 21:1-3; 22:4).

The Christian understanding of the gospel of Jesus Christ has been shaped decisively by these Pentateuchal texts. Abraham's response to God's command to sacrifice his "only son" is echoed in the Passion narratives of the Gospels. Jesus, like Israel, is called "out of Egypt" and tempted in the wilderness (Matt 2:15; 4:1-11). His being "lifted up" recalls Moses' lifting up the snake in the wilderness, which brought healing to the community of faith (John 3:14). He not only celebrates the Passover (Mark 14:12-25; Matt 26:28) but, in a radical theological extension, is himself identified as the "paschal lamb" (1 Cor 5:7; 11:25) and the "spiritual rock" who followed Israel in the wilderness (1 Cor 10:4). He assumes the role of a new Moses as he teaches his disciples from the mountain (Matthew 5–7). And, in the most remarkable move of all, Israel's God "tabernacles" in his very person (John 1:14). Drawing upon all sorts of existing interpretive vehicles, the New Testament writers use the Pentateuch to interpret *and* proclaim God's act in Jesus.

Theologies of various sorts have drawn on these Pentateuchal texts with abandon, from understandings of creation and human sinfulness to theories of atonement and the sacraments to issues of divine agency and human responsibility to ethical systems to more recent theologies of liberation from communities that know what oppression is all about. Christians understand their sinfulness in terms not unlike those mentioned in Genesis 3, know deeply in their own being the meaning of the cry, "Let my people go," and make their confession of faith in Abrahamic terms, "And he believed the LORD; and the LORD reckoned it to him as righteousness" (Gen 15:6). In view of such experience, the Pentateuch's witness to God's character remains integral to the testimony of every generation: "A God merciful and gracious, slow to anger, and abounding in steadfast love and faithfulness" (Exod 34:6). The God of Israel is our God; Israel's confessions and songs have become ours.

THE STUDY OF THE PENTATEUCH

An interesting combination of factors enlivens current study of the Pentateuch. On the one hand, the Pentateuch continues to enjoy a high status in those communities for whom the Bible is authoritative. Also, newly framed literary approaches in the academy have generated a vigorous interest in the narratives in particular. On the other hand, critical study is in disarray. Long-standing hypotheses have been found wanting, and no comprehensive alternative has yet captured the field. Even more, the continuing religious value of some texts has been questioned in view of their problematic perspectives on matters as diverse as the environment, the role of women, and the age of the universe.

A brief survey of basic approaches to Old Testament study, in which the study of the Pentateuch participates, will give some

sense of these developments. We use the following threefold outline as a convenient ordering of the discussion: the world behind
the text; the world within the text; the world in front of the text.[2]

The World Behind the Text

This phrase represents *author*-centered approaches, focused
on the *production* of the text. The meaning of the text is what the
author intended and can be discovered within the text itself. This
is commonly called the historical-critical method (or historical
criticism) and includes such approaches as source criticism, textual criticism, tradition criticism, form criticism, redaction criti-
cism, canonical criticism; historiography (the history of Israel in
its ancient Near Eastern setting); various sociological and anthropological approaches; and history of religions (comparison of
Israel's religion with other ancient Near Eastern religious traditions). The historical-critical method has been the dominant
approach to the Pentateuch from the late-eighteenth century to
the last third of the twentieth century. Hence, for introductory
purposes, we will give more attention to it than to other
approaches. But in subsequent chapters we will not often pursue
historical matters, the reasons for which will become evident as
we proceed.

Generally for this approach, the text is to be read as a *historical* document, the result of a complex historical process, wherein
it was shaped by the circumstances of the times and places in
which it was produced. The goal is the fullest *description* of the
world of the author(s) as is possible, on the basis of which one
can determine what the text *meant*. In pursuance of these tasks,
one must seek to understand as much of that ancient world as
possible—language, history, society and culture, literary conventions, and religious ideas and institutions.

The word "historical" is used in three basic senses, which give
shape to differing but related tasks:[3] (1) the history *in* the text,
that is, the story of Israel as the Bible itself tells it; (2) the history
behind the text, that is, the actual history of Israel as it can be
reconstructed on the basis of biblical and extrabiblical data. The
assumption is that the Bible itself does not tell us all that can be
known about this history nor does it portray this history in a
straightforward way; and (3) the history *of* the text, that is, the
origins and formation of the biblical literature as it has developed

over time. This would include two related components: (a) the first is the history of the literature, that is, how it evolved in the hands of authors and editors. Texts are often composite, having reached their present (= canonical) form in stages over a period of time; (b) the second is the history of interpretation, that is, the varying ways in which these authors and editors expressed the significance of the past (e.g., the Exodus) in the texts they were transmitting to a new generation.

This approach makes clear that reading the Bible is a cross-cultural experience; it exposes interpreters to a world that is other than our own, helping break us out of our cultural insularity, our narrow visions, and our limited experience. Such study informs readers about matters of content (e.g., events, persons, customs) that the author assumed the ancient reader knew and hence did not have to explain. Moreover, such an approach offers students an embodied text, having to do with real-life situations in a world other than our own. From this perspective, postbiblical communities of faith may more readily see continuities (and challenging discontinuities!) between that time and their own.

But this approach also complicates biblical study. The Bible can become simply another ancient artifact. Such an approach tends to stress the distance of the text from our world, the gulf between the past and present, a gulf that must be bridged for any contemporary appropriation. This is sometimes expressed in the phrases "what it *meant*" and "what it *means*" (see below). This raises a major interpretive issue: What is the nature of this bridge (often called "hermeneutics")? Interpreters have to traverse a bridge in both directions if they are going to get from then to now, but first they have to build the bridge or (more commonly) walk across someone else's construction. This is a difficult enterprise and can be discouraging to readers.

Such an approach has also neglected the treatment of the text as it now stands in favor of a search for origins. It assumes that what the text meant can be retrieved from an original setting, and that this meaning is to be privileged. In this process it often has been thought that an objective and neutral historical analysis is possible, insufficiently recognizing that the historian's own perspective deeply affects such an analysis. Moreover, a premium is placed on the use of a proper methodology, which tends to place the scholar (and those who appeal to such scholarship) on a pedestal and to privilege their interpretations. At least implicitly, it expects readers to become informed critics before they can claim any kind of confidence in biblical interpretation. In this and other ways it has neglected the reader (see below). Generally, such critics are probably more confident in their historical statements than they ought to be. The available historical data is actually quite sparse and difficult to interpret. Historical studies of Israel and its literature become dated quickly.

We survey here only three historical approaches, important not least because they have dominated the study of the Pentateuch over the last two centuries. The first two sections pertain to the third use of the word "historical" noted above; the third section to the second use.[4]

1. *Source Criticism.* Long the dominant scholarly approach to the Pentateuch, source criticism is a literary-historical analysis that seeks to determine the origins of a text, and hence focuses on such questions as authorship, the oral and written sources used, and the editorial stages through which it may have passed.

For centuries the author of the Pentateuch was assumed to be Moses. Questions about this tradition began to be raised in medieval and Reformation times. These questions were prompted by difficulties within the text itself (anachronisms; changes in style and vocabulary; inconsistencies; and repetitions or doublets), as well as the witness that sources were used in ancient times (see Num 21:14, 27; cf. Josh 10:13). This analysis eventually led many to deny authorship to Moses; this viewpoint is now so commonplace that voices to the contrary sound like special pleading. At the same time, it should be made clear that this source-critical approach often has been undertaken by persons interested in the religious and theological value of these texts.

Two basic tasks are involved in discerning sources: (1) literary observations. For example, more than one hundred doublets exist in the Pentateuch (cf. Lev 11:2-23 with Deut 14:4-20); or, shifts occur in vocabulary usage, such as names for God (cf. the use of the name Yahweh [= Lord] in Exod 6:2-3 and Gen 4:26), which became a key basis for delineating multiple sources; or, shifts in style and perspective (cf. Genesis with Deuteronomy). (2) the correlation of such sources with the development of ideas and institutions in other Old Testament literature, e.g., the bulk of

Deuteronomy appears to be the basis for the reform of Josiah in 2 Kings 22–23.

The classical formulation that resulted, associated especially with Julius Wellhausen,[5] spoke of four major sources—Yahwist (J), Elohist (E), Deuteronomist (D), and Priestly (P)—with some additional texts (e.g., Genesis 14; 49). These sources, from persons with different institutional bases and ideological commitments, were dated from the ninth to the fifth century BCE; they were gradually interwoven with one another over this time by a series of redactors. While debates about the unity, scope, and dating of these sources have been ongoing, the basic shape of this "documentary hypothesis" was fundamental to most studies of the Pentateuch until quite recently, and many scholars still work from this perspective.[6]

Especially sharp challenges have been brought to bear against this hypothesis (and other historical approaches) in the last generation. More conservative scholars (in Judaism and Christianity) have always been critical, but their objections were too often grounded in a view of the Bible and its inspiration rather than in an analysis of the texts themselves. Penetrating challenges have also been generated from within critical scholarship: the high level of expected coherence in thought and style (with atomistic results); the priority given to historical study and the search for origins—for what lies behind the text rather than in (and in front of) the text; the speculative nature of the sociohistorical setting thought to be reflected in the sources; the scope of the sources and their assumed continuity across the entire Pentateuch (less comprehensive proposals have been made); the nature and extent of the editorial work (e.g., some have argued for a more extensive Deuteronomic editing of Genesis–Numbers). As a result, source-critical work is presently in a state of disarray, with no consensus in sight.

Generally, it can be said that one basic result of source-critical study remains in place: the Pentateuch is a composite work that grew over the course of a half millennium or more. In addition, the identification of the Priestly material (and to a lesser degree the Deuteronomic) is agreed upon to a great extent.

2. *Form Criticism and History of Traditions.* A new direction in Pentateuchal study was initiated by the work of Hermann Gunkel on Genesis.[7] He moved away from a focus on larger, written

sources (without setting them aside) to smaller units of oral tradition that lay behind them. He assessed texts in terms of the types of literature or genres represented (e.g., legend, genealogy) and the social situations in which they were produced and functioned (e.g., worship, family setting) rather than individual authors and their intentions. He was not always clear how "oral literature" and written composition are to be related, but writers probably often used both oral and written sources; they did not simply commit oral materials to writing.

The two primary genres in the Pentateuch are law and narrative. While they are at times interwoven, they are not evenly distributed. Narrative predominates in the first third of the Pentateuch (Genesis–Exodus 19), while collections of law dominate Leviticus and Deuteronomy. The naming of the narratives more precisely—e.g., saga, legend—has proved difficult. The word "story" is common, but imprecise and ambiguous. The designation "theological narrative" helpfully indicates that this literature is an admixture of Israel's story and God's story, and certain texts strongly evidence such interests (e.g., Gen 12:1-3; 22:1-18). In some texts, a hortatory rhetoric is prominent (e.g., Deuteronomy 8), with a concern to move heart and will as well as the mind. In addition, genealogies (especially in Genesis) and poetic pieces (e.g., Genesis 49; Exodus 15) are represented.

Form-critical analysis remains an important enterprise in current Pentateuchal study, particularly with respect to delineating types of literature and the role they play within the present text.

Building upon the results of both source- and form-critical study, a history of traditions approach was developed; the work of Gerhard von Rad was especially influential.[8] He sought to track the growth of the Pentateuchal traditions from their earliest discernible preliterary stage to their latest literary stage. Basic to his proposal is the existence of certain "creeds" (e.g., Deut 26:5-9; Josh 24:2-13) used at sanctuaries in pre-monarchical Israel to confess the basic "acts of God." These confessional elements constituted an outline for what in time became the Hexateuch (= the Pentateuch plus Joshua). This outline, a "Hexateuch in miniature," was filled out over the years by preachers and teachers who related this confession to the ongoing life of the people. Hence, a liturgical setting was the primary matrix for the ongoing transmission and growth of these traditions; liturgy has given a decisive

27

shape to this literature. The next stages of growth are related to the written sources, of which J is especially important. The Yahwist gave Israel's story a universal context by prefacing segments of Genesis 1–11, tied the ancestral stories together with the theme of promise-fulfillment (see Gen 12:1-3), and linked the creedal ("gospel") material with the giving of the law at Sinai (which had been separately transmitted during the early years). Other sources, with theological interests, were used to supplement and edit this material over succeeding centuries (e.g., E and P).

Two additional studies may be noted. Martin Noth, a contemporary of von Rad, set about the same task.[9] He considered the Yahwist to be less important, believing that the basic framework and major themes of the Pentateuch were in place prior to the major sources (in an oral or written source he called G, *Grundschrift*). The work of Albrecht Alt, who focused on Pentateuchal law, was also influential.[10] He considered the law of the apodictic type (e.g., the Decalogue), as distinguished from case law, to have been developed and used in Israel's worship. Hence, from several perspectives, worship came to be seen as the primary matrix for the development of a significant portion of the Pentateuch.

Although discussions continue on many fronts, one lasting effect of this approach is the recognition that the Pentateuch has been decisively shaped by religious and theological interests and institutions. The extent to which practitioners had their hand in this process may be debated (it is most evident in the hortatory rhetoric of Deuteronomy and texts such as Exodus 12), but persons of faith were primarily responsible for shaping and reshaping these traditions in order to speak a word of/about God to successive communities of faith.

The study of Deuteronomy has taken a somewhat separate route from that of the other major sources. Deuteronomy has long been associated with the book of the law that shaped the reform of Josiah in the late-seventh century BCE (see 2 Kings 22–23). But scholars such as Martin Noth have extended this conversation.[11] On the basis of literary and theological similarities between Deuteronomy and Dtr (= Joshua, Judges, Samuel, Kings), and the uncommon presence of Deuteronomic material in Genesis–Numbers (often called the Tetrateuch), he associated Deuteronomy more with the books that follow than with those that precede. Deuteronomy may have served as a preface to Dtr (with Deut 1:1–4:40 as the introduction to the entire corpus). Sometime in the postexilic period, Deuteronomy, because it focused on the law and its mediator Moses, was joined with the Tetrateuch (with certain texts transferred from the end of Numbers to the end of Deuteronomy). This hypothesis remains a dominant approach to the Deuteronomic literature.

3. *History, Faith, and Historiography.* Questions regarding the extent to which these texts reflect what actually happened in Israel's early history have generated an animated and conflicted conversation. No blanket statement can be made about the Pentateuch as a whole; every text must be examined in itself to determine historicity. The results have been somewhat mixed, with little consensus among scholars regarding the extent to which these texts are historically reliable. Such conclusions have made some readers nervous, for the authority of the Bible seems thereby to be called into question. Yet, the truth value of biblical texts is not necessarily related to their historicity (witness parables, for example).

Historians use various criteria to evaluate the reliability of data for reconstructing the past. Among the more important factors are discernible purpose(s) for which the material was written, the types of literature represented, the complexities of transmission histories, and the congruity with external evidence unearthed by archaeologists.[12] Some reflections on these criteria may be helpful.

These texts are not historical narrative, at least in any modern sense. They have not been written to reconstruct the history of Israel, using historiographical methods. Given this reality, readers, with their (legitimate) interest in historiographical matters, should recognize that they use these texts in a way they were not intended to be used. For example, the language of error/inaccuracy ought not be used to devalue these texts, just as one would not use it to misprize the imaginative retelling of biblical stories for children. Israelites likely thought that these traditions were inherited from ancient times, but no evidence exists that they evaluated them in terms of issues of historicity. The narrators certainly transmitted matters that did not correspond to the facts, but this reality should be evaluated in terms of purposes that were not historiographical.

At the same time, it is just as clear that these texts are concerned to tell a story of the past, namely, the story of Israel's origins and early life (and those of other peoples). The reader begins deeply in the past and moves along a time line toward the land settlement, with a chronological interest evident all along the way. Generally speaking, however, this chronology is probably fictive, evident especially in the precision of the chronological schematic (though the details are not always clear; cf. Gen 15:13, 16; Exod 12:40; Gal 3:17). Such an assessment of the schematic is suggested by the fact that the Hebrew Bible's chronology differs from that of the Septuagint and that of the Samaritan Pentateuch. These differences point to the ongoing workings of special interests on these chronologies and complicate efforts to decipher the details. Some figures to be noted: the Hebrew Bible counts 1,946 years from the creation to the birth of Abraham (Gen 11:26); 2,666 years to the Exodus (is it important that this is 2/3 of 4,000?), and 40 more years to the death of Moses, for a total of 2,706 years.[13]

The flow of time through the Pentateuch is generally coherent, but very uneven. The chronology of Genesis is laid out in terms of over 2,000 years. On the other hand, Deuteronomy covers only twenty-four hours (1:3; 32:48-50). In between, the long stretch from Exod 19:1 through Leviticus to Num 10:11 covers almost twelve months. These varying temporal intensities affect the readers' experience of the narrative, slowing them down at times to ponder what is at stake. While the Pentateuch is fundamentally concerned with telling a story of the past, the reader is thereby invited to consider more than questions of origins and early ancestral experiences.

Two representative, if now somewhat dated, efforts to assess the historical value of these texts are those of Martin Noth and John Bright.[14] Noth's conclusions were very negative regarding the historicity of these materials; for example, he argued that the only certain thing to be reported about Moses was his burial. His conclusions have been criticized from various angles, not least his failure to ask how Moses came to have such an important role, and how likely it would be that so much of Israel's early history was lacking in genuine memories. John Bright was more optimistic regarding the historical value of these texts, but even he was reticent to claim too much (e.g., that Abraham, Isaac, and Jacob were actually related). His efforts have been faulted for a too easy correlation between the biblical texts and archaeological data.[15]

Congruity with such external data is another important factor in assessing the value of texts for historiographical purposes. It needs to be asked whether such data corroborates, or stands over against, the biblical traditions. A period of some confidence (mid-twentieth century) in the basic historicity of these texts within the second millennium BCE has faded in recent years in view of the analysis of the texts themselves and the interpretation of putative archaeological evidence. Various kinds of ancient Near Eastern data, thought to be parallel to names, customs, and modes of life in these texts, have at times been overinterpreted. Certainly no details in the Pentateuchal texts have been corroborated and many difficulties remain. It is wise to remember that archaeological findings do not prove (or disprove) the *truth* of the Bible; whatever correspondences may be found with respect to factual data, no external corroboration can be found regarding *meaning* (e.g., that God was active). But, certainly, some genuine memories of Israel's early history have been preserved; however, it is exceptionally difficult to discern what these might be.

How important for faith is it that the matters reported in these texts happened? Some interpreters make no distinctions among biblical texts at this point; the historicity of every matter, down to the details of the most private of conversations, carry equal weight for faith. Yet, such an approach stands at odds with that of the biblical writers themselves; they give us warrant to make distinctions among events. They single out certain events as being constitutive of the community, and hence important for faith. References to such events (e.g., the Exodus), unlike most others, have been incorporated into confessional statements (e.g., Deut 26:5-9) and integrated again and again into the community's basic theological reflections.

The result is that the Pentateuch contains a very mixed set of materials from a historical perspective. It is clear that these texts are placed chronologically in the time before Israel entered Canaan (before 1200 BCE or so), and they are presented as moving steadily toward that objective, both in terms of the sequencing of events and in theological terms (as promises moving toward fulfillment). Moreover, the story is remarkably free of pretense, describing the Israelite ancestors in terms that are often unattractive. These texts reflect what thoughtful Israelites at various times considered the meaning(s) of that story to be, and they

are historical at least in that sense. Though much of this reflection certainly stems from times *subsequent* to the entry into
Canaan, important continuities with earlier times are probably
present. At the same time, in such a reflective process, the
authors and editors no doubt used their imaginations freely (e.g.,
the words of a private conversation) in the ongoing retelling
process. But, even where the judgment of the historiographers
may be negative regarding historicity, the material retains its
import as a word of/about God.

The World Within the Text

In contrast to the historical-critical method that focuses on the
development and background of the text, other approaches are *text*-
centered, focused on the *product,* the text itself. For text-centered
methods, meaning is inherent in the text itself and can be discerned
by a careful analysis of how the textual features work together. This
approach (I use the singular for convenience; there are various
approaches) is often called the new literary criticism, and includes
various strategies that have not yet been defined precisely in relation to one another (e.g., rhetorical criticism and structuralism).
This approach emerged in the middle of the twentieth century
within biblical studies and has gained considerable strength.[16]

This approach honors the text as text, as it presently exists in
its own right, apart from historical issues that may be raised,
including authorship. The text is autonomous, self-standing,
independent of any external world; it has its own internal world
that requires attention, its own voice (not an author's) with which
it speaks. Rather than treating the text in an atomistic way, as a
composite of disparate pieces from various times and places, the
text is accepted as a unified entity, an organic and coherent
whole. The various repetitions, disjunctions, and inconsistencies
of the text (discerned from a historical approach) are, rather, evidence of a developed literary craft. The text now has a life of its
own and readers must come to terms with it as such.

This approach, rather than investigating how the text may have
originated and evolved through the years (a diachronic concern),
studies the text in its present form (a synchronic concern). But
this approach does share with historical criticism the assumption
that there is one textual meaning, and that with the proper
research tools one can discover and retrieve that meaning. This

meaning, however, is not to be associated with an author in an ancient setting; it is solely *inherent in* the text. One recognizes meaning by seeing how a text works, how its various literary and rhetorical features function in relation to one another to present an artistic whole. Special attention is given to such matters as language and style, surface and deep structures of the text, rhetorical devices, literary genres, narratological features such as repetition, irony, plot, depiction of characters, and especially point of view (of the characters and narrator, e.g., in Gen 18:1-2, the narrator speaks of the appearance of the Lord, Abraham sees three men). If relationships to the ancient world are drawn into the conversation, they have to do with literary and rhetorical features that may be held in common.

Unlike the historical method, this approach does not have the problem of a gulf between past and present. The meaning of the text is not something from the past that one seeks to bring into the present; the meaning of the text is always as contemporary as the reader. Yet, while the historical gap is not explicitly present, the text is still recognized as an ancient document (say, in the use of the Hebrew language). Even so, because this approach is so focused on the text itself, it has the capacity to surface latent meaning possibilities more immediately than the historical approach has been able to do.

At the same time, difficulties with this approach have begun to surface. As with historical criticism, a text-centered approach can be methodologically imperialistic, as if this were now the only real way to read texts. Its formalistic methods have contributed to an impression that this is a more objective approach, and that if one were only to learn and apply the various methods in rigorous fashion, one could arrive at *the* meaning of the text. But this could fail to recognize the social location of the interpreter, as well as that of the voice in the text; both are deeply informed by their life situations, gender and class, and philosophical and theological biases of one kind or another. Moreover, the inattention to historical realities, the *lack* of a gulf between past and present, presents its own problems. It can, for example, lead to an understanding of the text as disembodied, unrelated to the complexities and ambiguities, the joys and sorrows of real life. Generally, this approach diminishes both author and reader in favor of precision in analysis of the text's literary features.

Because this approach is relatively new, and is so focused on the study of individual texts, few examples of such a study exist for the entire Pentateuch.[17]

The World in Front of the Text

In contrast to author-centered and text-centered approaches, a *reader*-centered approach has emerged; it focuses on the *reception* of the text or, more precisely, on the interaction between reader and text. Texts are not autonomous, independent of those who read them, and cannot communicate without a reader. Hence, meaning is neither found in the mind of the author nor is it inherent in the text; it is the result of the conversation between text and reader. So, no single meaning is to be sought in the text; indeed, meaning changes over time, even for the same reader, because readers change. Meanings of texts, then, will always be to some degree open-ended; they are not fixed and stable. One form of this approach is reader-response criticism; it is only in its infancy in biblical studies.[18]

Everyone who opens the Bible is a reader, but that obvious point has seldom been explored. While the act of reading is held in common by all, there are many different types of readers. I note three here: (a) the implied reader, the one for whom the text is written (see next chapter). This reader is inferred from data within the text itself (in a similar way one speaks of an implied author); (b) the historical reader, the reader who would have read the text in ancient times, which may correspond to the implied reader in many ways; (c) readers in every postbiblical generation. The latter are the special concern of reader-response criticism.

Texts exert an influence on their readers, on their thinking, speaking, and living. Key questions for reader response are these: How does language function in the text to exert such influence, to promote one or another kind of impact on the reader? What do the rhetorical strategies employed do, or seek to do, to the reader? Do they give the reader information, persuade the reader regarding a point of view, make judgments on opinions or behavior, or move the reader to action? How do such strategies affect the lives of readers and the various relationships in which they are enmeshed? Then, more broadly, How is one to evaluate such readings, and what role do readers' communities play in this

34

process? Do the resultant readings make for life, well-being, and the flourishing of individuals and communities?

This approach is attentive to the fact that the text is filled with polysemic words (having more than one meaning), metaphors, ambiguities of grammar and expression (cf. translations of Gen 1:1), and silences or gaps of various kinds (e.g., Exod 4:24-26). These realities not only make the reader necessary in order to make sense of the text, but in deciding about such matters, the reader participates in the making of meaning. In such interpretive acts, readers can never step outside of themselves or their situation, and hence what they bring to the text becomes a part of the meaning of the text. Eisegesis (reading *into* the text) has long been denounced in favor of exegesis (reading *out of* the text), but the truth of the matter is that both moves are employed in every readerly act. Indeed, if one ignores this subjective dimension of the interpretive process, one will uncritically transmit or promote interpretations that are inevitably informed by one ideology or another. All interpreters are having to learn anew that they are to read from within an explicit recognition of their own history and social location.

This approach takes all readers seriously, honors what they bring to the task, and includes them as full participants in the task of making meaning. One of the effects of this is that formerly marginalized and silenced readers—women, minorities, and Third World audiences—are getting their readings of texts into the public domain and traditional specialists are having to attend to such readings. At the same time, this approach does not deny the important role that specialists can play in certain aspects of interpretation (see the constraints below).

But do no constraints on meaning possibilities exist? Are there as many readings as there are readers? At least three limiting factors can be considered; they show that a text cannot mean anything just because it can mean many things.

1. *The text itself.* With its distinctive features, the text itself influences readings in certain directions and not others. Texts do shape readers; readers are not in full control of meanings nor do they create them out of whole cloth. But texts are not as stable as one might think; the above-noted gaps and ambiguities affect interpretation greatly. Texts can be a source of instability and the proliferation of Bible translations reflects this reality.

2. *Historical background information.* The text was shaped by

certain realities in the culture within which it was produced—events, persons, social and political realities—knowledge of which is often assumed by the author. Such knowledge, which may be productive of insight, also provides constraints on textual meanings, though it is not as stable as one might like; scholarly historical constructions often are speculative and the data often ambiguous and drawn into imaginative retellings.

3. *The many and diverse communities* within which texts and readers reside. As for *texts,* they are not autonomous (as noted), but exist only in a web of community beliefs about the Bible or the meaning of particular texts. Texts can no longer be read as if for the first time. As for *readers,* they are shaped by the diverse communities to which they belong and so are their readings. Moreover, much common ground has been achieved in both church and academy regarding interpretive conventions (e.g., form criticism) and meanings of texts, and this reduces, consciously or unconsciously, the variety of possible meanings. But openness to various meanings in texts enables more new insights, gives more room for the play of the imagination, encourages conversation, and provides additional avenues in and through which the Word of God can address people in increasingly diverse contexts.[19]

These newer text-oriented and reader-oriented approaches have not swept aside all interest in historical factors that have shaped the present text. Indeed, many scholars think that these approaches should complement each other. This may prove to be the case, but just how this complementarity might be worked out remains to be seen. The following chapter proposes a way of reading the Pentateuch that draws on various approaches, especially those that are text-oriented and reader-oriented. But my interest is not in these approaches as such, nor in various theories that have been proposed, though these will inform my reading.

THE THEOLOGICAL TASK

My interest focuses on the basic content of the Pentateuch, especially what it says about God and the divine-human relationship. The word "theology" appropriately designates this content; by this I mean the theology *in* the text and not some overarching biblical theology (though the former would have implications for the latter).[20] I affirm Rolf Rendtorff's claim: "The Hebrew Bible is itself a theological book. That means that the Bible does not only *become* theological through interpretation by a later-elaborated theology, be it rabbinic or Christian; rather, it is possible and necessary to find the theological ideas and messages of the biblical texts themselves" (italics mine).[21]

The word "theology" has been suspect in biblical study, often because it is thought to introduce subjective factors into an "objective" or "descriptive" enterprise. But, in the last third of the twentieth century in particular, we have come to see that every person who works with the text, from whatever angle, introduces subjective factors, whether admitted or not. Theological analysis is not innately any more subjective than historical or literary study. We are learning that it is no longer appropriate to distinguish between what the text *meant* and what it *means,* and that the phrase "descriptive task" for theological (or any other) analysis can be deeply misleading. All questions asked of the text are contemporary questions and all results of our work with the text are, finally, *constructive.*

The theology in the text never surfaces on its own or in some "naked" form. The making of meaning, including theological meaning, is a product of the interaction of text and reader. Hence, any restatement or elucidation of a text's theology is a combination of the theology of the text and that of the reader. My theological work in this book, for example, will inevitably be informed by the fact that I am a Christian and a Lutheran, and read the works of certain theologians but not others. Yet, this is not to claim that just any theological interpretation of the text will do. The constraining factors noted above apply as much to theological analysis as to any other.

God-talk is introduced in Pentateuchal texts in several ways. The most common are those instances where God is the subject of a sentence in the narrative (e.g., Gen 12:1-3) or in the law (e.g., Exod 22:21-27). Interwoven with these references are "creedal" and generalized statements about God. One type of statement gathers claims about God that focus on divine acts (Deut 26:4-9). Another type of statement articulates these claims in more abstract ways: God is compassionate (Exod 22:27); gracious, merciful, slow to anger, and abounding in steadfast love (Exod 34:6-7; Num 14:18); holy (Lev 19:2); great, mighty, awesome, is not partial and takes no bribe, executes justice for the orphan and the widow, and loves the stranger (Deut 10:17-18). Such truth claims about God and the divine relationship to the world both convey certain convictions about God and provide internal direction for the meaning of other God references. That is, the God who is the subject of sentences in narrative or law is to be understood relative to these specific truth claims, while leaving room for developments in understanding.

The Pentateuch is an especially rich theological work, and I seek to show in the following chapter that theology plays a central role, not only with respect to the content of the Pentateuch but also regarding its very form and its rhetorical strategy.

CHAPTER 2

A PROPOSAL FOR READING THE PENTATEUCH

In this chapter, I draw especially on aspects of the text-oriented and reader-oriented approaches presented in the last chapter and propose a way of reading the Pentateuch that takes theological considerations especially into account. I begin with a discussion regarding the implied reader/audience of the Pentateuch and move to some reflections on the rhetorical strategy used to appeal to this audience, particularly as that is evident in the way the Pentateuch begins and ends.

This proposal assumes that any assessment of the Pentateuch's rhetorical strategy (and by this I mean any matter of style or content designed to contribute to the desired effect on readers) must be informed by theological considerations, indeed by the theological claims of the text (see conclusion of chapter 1). If a religious response is the effect desired from readers (see chapter 7 on Deuteronomy), then it ought not be surprising if theological claims play such a strategic role. The theology in the Pentateuch has a decisive role to play with respect to its form and its rhetorical strategy.

THE IMPLIED READER/AUDIENCE

What is meant when we speak of the implied reader(s) of the Pentateuch? These readers are the ones for whom the Pentateuch is written; theoretically, they could be actual (historical) readers or imagined ones. The Pentateuch—and here we leave aside readers of earlier forms of the Pentateuch—was written to have an effect on these readers. We as (real) readers seek to identify and describe these readers, the kind of effect on them the text seeks to have, and the rhetorical strategies used to accomplish it.

The identity of these readers is a literary construct; that is, it is inferred from the data within the text itself by readers such as you and me. This data will include or imply an assessment or interpretation of these readers (e.g., the state of their relationship with God). Once these readers have been identified from the textual data, links regarding these readers may then be established with data available from other sources (e.g., other biblical books); these readers may be historically identifiable.

The Pentateuch is shaped in such a way as to address these implied readers. Certain rhetorical strategies are employed to have an effect on them. What sorts of effects on these readers are possible? Three may be noted: (1) the reception of new information or a new perspective; (2) to be moved to think, speak, or act differently; (3) a religious response, wherein one is converted or comforted or challenged to a new appreciation of God or the divine-human relationship and its implications for life. The strategies and effects may be various in the Pentateuch, as we shall see, but the general objective is to bring about change in the readers, to create persons different from what they were before the reading took place.

It can be shown that the implied readers of the Pentateuch bear a family resemblance to the exiles in Babylon (587–538 BCE), but it seems just as clear that these exiles do not "exhaust" the identity of the implied readers; that is, the text stops short of such an explicit identification, though given many opportunities to do so. This lack of specificity leaves more room for other readers to hear themselves addressed. This analysis raises issues regarding these other readers of this text through the centuries and their relationship to the original implied readers. Generally, to the degree that postbiblical readers of the text find themselves addressed by it, the text may function in comparable ways. A full-scale analysis of the implied readers is not possible here, but I will note some general matters, and then seek to draw out some of the rhetorical strategies from a close look at the beginning and ending of the Pentateuch.

At the simplest level, the Pentateuch assumes that its readers are able to read texts and to read them in Hebrew. It is assumed that they will have certain general information in hand, for example, the basics of their social and religious heritage. Knowledge of key events, characters, customs, and traditions, including the law and certain features of the Mosaic tradition, are often presupposed.

At the same time, parenthetical comments inserted here and there suggest some loss of memory, both geographical and historical. A look at Deuteronomy, especially chaps. 1–4, may illustrate the point for the Pentateuch as a whole. The audience needs to be informed about certain details regarding the geography of Canaan (1:2; 3:9, 13; 4:48; 11:30; 34:3); note the need to specify the "neighboring regions" of Canaan (1:7; cf. 1:1) or certain boundary lines (3:16-17; cf. Num 13:13) or the location of places (Nebo, 32:49; Pisgah, 34:1). Moreover, historical notes are entered for information and clarification (2:10-12, 20-23; 3:11, 13-14; 4:44-49); the reference to Og's iron bed is archive-like (3:11). This is sufficient to suggest that the readers are spatially removed from Canaan and need prompting regarding geographical knowledge.

Other phrases suggest temporal distance. The recurrent phrase, "at that time" (2:34; 3:4, 23), with some detail regarding the extent of the capture (3:4-7), suggests some distance from the events. The charge not "to forget" or let such matters "slip from your mind all the days of your life" (4:9, 23) and to "call [blessings and curses] to mind" (30:1) manifests a concern about memory loss. The phrases "as you are now" (4:20) and "as it is still today" (4:38; cf. 5:3; 11:4; 3:14; 34:6) clearly indicate a later time; indeed, they suggest that readers may wonder whether peoplehood and land can still be claimed, perhaps evidence for a dispirited state of mind (see 31:6-8).

These texts are congruent with several others that have long been thought, on the basis of style, content, and perspective, to show signs of having been written after the destruction and exile of Judah in 587 BCE (Lev 26:27-44; Deut 4:25-31; 8:19-20;

28:36-37, 45-68; 29:20-28; 30:1-20; cf. 1 Kgs 8:46-53; 9:6-9; 2 Kgs 21:8-15). It seems likely that the implied readers of the Pentateuch had experienced the apostasy, the devastation of Jerusalem and its attendant losses and sufferings, and the deportation to Babylon (among other clues, the phrase "as is now the case," [29:28] suggests that they are now in fact in "another land"; cf. also the "you/your" in 30:1-10). The readers were now the remnant that had survived and had to tussle with the realities of exile, including apostasy, fear, distress, repentance, and wondering about the return to the land and the continuing validity of the divine promises. At the same time, the lack of an unassailable reference to the events of 587 BCE leaves the text open to readers who have experienced comparable events at *any* time and place (might the fall of Samaria in 721 BCE be an earlier instance?).

The rhetorical force of these texts regarding this future interweave elements of conditionality (if you are faithful or unfaithful, 30:15-20) and certainty, "when all these things have happened to you in time to come" (4:30). Indeed, they will return to the Lord in their distress and heed him (4:28-30). They are assured that they are still God's possession and that the land is still theirs, indeed it is theirs "for all time" (4:40). And, above all, they are assured that even if they forget, God will not forget them (4:31) and will gather them up and return them to the land (30:4-5).

Another rhetorical feature of Deuteronomy is a portrayal of the people of God that pushes beyond historical specifics and becomes applicable to *every generation of Israelites.* As 5:3 puts it, "Not with our ancestors did the LORD make this covenant, but *with us,* who are all of us here alive today" (italics mine). Every generation would understand that the "with us" applied to them and that they were the addressees of both the laws and the promises. Each generation was to place their hope in a God who would fulfill promises and make them dwell secure in the land (30:1-10).

This actualizing tendency (making the past real in every present time) is reinforced by the use of the second person pronoun in chaps. 1–11 (cf. also the "we/us" in chaps. 1–3). The distinction between old and new generation is made (1:35; 2:14), but at the same time it is collapsed. The "you" of the exodus (4:20) is also the "you" of the land settlement (4:5), and the "you" of the rebellion (1:26) is also the "you" of faithfulness (4:4). The same range of experience is ascribed to the "you" in chaps. 6–11 (e.g., 6:21-24; 7:15-18; 8:14-16; 9:7-24; 11:4-7). Everyone who is listening would understand themselves as *participants in all phases of this story*. Even more, the "you" includes not only the Israel that lives in the land, but the "you" that is dispossessed from the land (4:25-31; 8:20; 11:17) and the "you" that lives through the exile and is restored to the land (30:1, 3, 9)! In other words, even though Moses is speaking to one (the new) generation, the "you" cuts across the generations. It is likened to the "with us" of 5:3; everyone is to recognize this story as their story.

To such material may be linked texts associated with Israel's worship life. One example is the "place the LORD will choose" (see 12:1-32). It is commonly identified with Jerusalem; yet, the lack of specific reference makes it more likely that the identity of the place has been left purposely open-ended so that the central sanctuary of any generation would fit (Jerusalem is only one). Another example is the Passover (16:1-8), where the "remembering" effects participation in the exodus for "you."

The following sections will support and fill out this discussion. My approach is to take a close look at the beginning of the Pentateuch and its ending, and the way they are related to each other. At the same time, I will pursue clues that this material may give for discerning how readers might experience these texts in view of the rhetorical strategies employed. Questions to keep in mind include: What is the relationship of the readers to the inherited tradition? Do they, for example, doubt its continuing power for daily life? What words give evidence of a certain self-understanding? To what are appeals made? What basic theological categories are assumed (e.g., God)? Is there evidence of a crisis in their situation? Where might controversies be centered? Is the audience in need of encouragement or admonition or both? For what kind of audience would such a beginning and ending be especially suitable?

THE SENSE OF A BEGINNING

The beginning of the Pentateuch (Genesis 1–11), as with any effective literary work, is key to a proper discernment of its rhetorical strategy and its probable effect on readers. How would the reader experience this "opener"? It seems clear that this material is not laid out simply to give the reader some basic information about the world or the beginnings of things. Rather, the strategy is to catch the reader up into *a universal frame of reference*. The story does not begin with Israel or the situation of the implied (or any other) reader or even with the human race, initially. The readers are invited to view a screen that is cosmic in its scope and to engage in an act of the imagination that carries them beyond—way beyond—their little corner of the world, wherever that may be.

In the service of this strategy, the opening chapters present a rhythmic interweaving of story and genealogy that focuses the mind on certain recurring images, especially those of God and the world. These images set the tone and direction for *reading all that follows*. Their canonical placement at the beginning argues for a certain way of reading the Pentateuch when it speaks of God, world, and their relationship. One of the remarkable features of Genesis 1–11 is that the basic images of God that readers will encounter in the rest of the Pentateuch are introduced before there was an Israel. This is a witness to the kind of God who is active in the world more generally, not just in Israel. New images or ideas may well emerge beyond these chapters (e.g., Exod 34:6-7), but the reader is to deal with them against the backdrop provided by the beginning.

God as Creator

One of the Pentateuch's most basic assumptions about the readers is that God does not have to be introduced (1:1). Moreover, the name Yahweh is assumed to be known (2:4). This God whom they know is first of all presented as a creator.[1] To begin the Pentateuch with powerful images of the Creator and the creation accomplishes several things.

1. It reflects the actual order of divine activity in the world. God was at work in the world and in the lives of all creatures on behalf of God's creational purposes long before Israel came into being or articulated what creation was all about.

2. It gives priority of place to God's actual engagement with the world, rather than to human knowledge of such divine activity. Human beings—as individuals or communities—receive life from the Creator quite apart from any knowledge of its source.

Israel's later understandings of creation only "catch up" with what God has long been about in the world.

3. It parallels the human experience of God's activity. God's promissory and redemptive activity does not occur in a vacuum, but in a context shaped by the life-giving and life-enhancing work of the Creator. God's work in creation is necessary for there to be a people whom God can redeem and a context within which they can live well. For example, the growth of Israel *in Egypt* is seen as a fulfillment of God's word in creation (Exod 1:7; Gen 1:28).

4. It demonstrates that God's work in the world has to do with more than human beings. Most of God's activity in Genesis 1 involves the creation of that which is other than human; indeed, God involves the nonhuman in creative activity (1:11, 20, 22, 24). Even more, the human and nonhuman orders are deeply integrated, so that, for example, human sin has devastating effects on the nonhuman world ("thorns and thistles," 3:17; the flood). Moreover, the nonhuman creatures are caught up in God's saving work (6:19–7:3), God's remembering (8:1), and God's promising (9:10). Readers of the rest of the Pentateuch should be attuned to the important place of the nonhuman in God's economy. One need only mention the plagues, the role of the nonhuman as mediator of God's delivering activity in the exodus, the recreative activity of God in the wilderness, and the pyrotechnics on Mt. Sinai.

5. It makes clear the intentions of God's redemptive work. The opening chapters demonstrate that God's purposes in redemption are not finally centered on Israel; they are universal in scope. God's redemption of Israel serves the divine intention with respect to the creation in its entirety. This universal mission informs more of what the Pentateuch is about than has been commonly recognized.

Israel comes on the scene only within the context of all the nations/families of the earth (Genesis 10–11); Israel's election and reception of the divine promises are specifically tied back into this world family in Gen 12:1-3, "in you all the families of the earth shall be blessed." All these families are the ultimate concern of God; they are the ones who stand in need of the blessing (especially in view of sin and its effects). The ancestral narrative is punctuated with this divine mission in and through Israel (18:18; 22:18; 26:4; 28:14), and this is concretely shown in the various interactions between Israel's progenitors and virtually every people in Israel's environs.[2]

While the rest of the Pentateuch focuses on the people of Israel, God's mission continues to be more broadly conceived. God's actions for Israel and against the Egyptians are "to make my name resound through all the earth" (Exod 9:16). The knowledge of God and the glorification of God before the Egyptians, indeed all the earth, are fundamental divine objectives (cf. 8:10, 22; 9:14, 29; 14:4). God's liberating actions at the sea affect other peoples (15:14-16) and God's reign is established over all the earth (15:18). Israel is given a vocation among the nations to function as a priest does within a religious community, "for all the earth is mine" (Exod 19:5-6 RSV), and "all the people among whom you live shall see the work of the LORD" (Exod 34:10). Even the giving of the law is related to the impact it might have on the larger world (Deut 4:6-8), and Israel's disobedience of the law will occasion wonderment among the nations (Deut 29:24-28). Note also God's work of blessing through the outsider, Balaam (Numbers 22–24).

God as an Electing God

God's electing activity does not begin with Abraham. Electing is set in universal terms as a basic way in which God chooses to work in the world. One, God chooses Abel's offering rather than Cain's (4:4-5); this divine choice of the younger over the elder brother relates to issues of primogeniture in the chapters that follow, as God chooses Isaac rather than Ishmael, and Jacob rather than Esau (cf. also 38:27-30; 48:13-14). In each case, the divine choice generates conflict among people who are not able to handle that very well. Two, God chooses Noah (Gen 6:8-9) as the one to be saved from the flood. With him God begins again with the human family and enters into covenant. As such, God's electing activity is not an end in itself; God elects for the purpose of preserving the creation by keeping it alive.

Such purposes of life and well-being for the entire creation are continued and brought into sharper focus in God's election of Abraham/Israel. God's choice of Israel in love and in order to keep the oath to its ancestors (Deut 7:6-8) is so that "you may live, and that it may go well with you, and that you may live long in the land that you are to possess" (Deut 5:33; cf. 6:24). As noted above,

Israel's election is for the sake of the world. God's initially exclusive move in choosing Abraham/ Israel is for the sake of a maximally inclusive end.

God as Savior

A related theme set from the beginning is the image of God as Savior; God delivers both human beings and animals from the flood (see especially 8:1). This puts in place from the start a fundamental way in which God chooses to relate to the world as a whole. Given human sinfulness and the dire effects let loose in God's creation, God chooses to be a savior. Even more, this shows that God is active in saving ways out and about in the creation independent of Israel and the mediation of the community of faith. Generally, God enters into salvific activity especially on behalf of those who are oppressed or otherwise disadvantaged.

The God who is savior of the world is the savior of Israel, and this will center the rest of the Pentateuch. Just how this specific saving activity is to be related to God's more universal saving action will need attention along the way. God acts in saving ways on behalf of the ancestors (e.g., Gen 14:20), but especially in delivering Israel from bondage in Egypt (Exod 3:8; 6:6; 14:30; 18:11). This God continues to deliver the people all along their wilderness journey and can be counted on to be their savior from enemies (cf. Deut 33:29), including those whom it encounters as it enters into the promised land. In addition, this theme of divine saving action, especially on behalf of the less fortunate, informs the structures of the law, and to such an extent that God binds himself to the Torah in acting on their behalf (Exod 22:21-27).

The God of the Covenant Promise

The God of the covenant promise constitutes a basic image for all that follows. After the flood, God makes a covenant with Noah and all flesh (9:8-17; cf. 8:21-22). This is a unilateral covenant with the entire creation, human and nonhuman, in which God binds himself—thereby limiting the divine options—with respect to the future: not to destroy the earth in floodlike ways again. Covenant is thus introduced into the narrative as a word with universal associations; God is active in this way, with creation quite apart from Israel. In the wake of the flood, God decides to go with the world, come what may in the way of human wickedness. If human beings are to live, they must be undergirded by the divine promise (see Exod 34:9 for a comparable move with Israel).[3] This covenant continues to function for Israel as an illustration of the inviolability of God's promises (see Isa 54:9-10; Jer 31:35-36; 33:20-26).

The God who makes covenant with Abraham/Israel is a God who has already established a promissory relationship with the creation. The latter covenant makes all other covenants possible, for without it the creation would not be preserved alive. Even more, God's covenant with Abraham/Israel is grounded in this prior promise, revealing as it does God's most basic way of relating to the world—in commitment and patience and mercy, not in anger. The covenants that God makes later are as good as God is here revealed to be.

The covenant with Noah and all flesh is revealing of the basic structure within which subsequent covenants occur: God elects (6:8); God saves (6:18; 8:1); human beings respond in worship and faith (8:20); and only then does God establish covenant. This fourfold structure is characteristic of God's covenants with Abraham (12:1-3; 12:10-20 and 14:20; 15:6; 15:18), with Israel (the covenant is not made until Exodus 24), and even with David (2 Samuel 7).

God as One Who Blesses

Blessing is given creationwide scope from the beginning. Blessing is integral to God's creative action, with respect to both animals and human beings (1:22, 28), and even the temporal structures of the created order (2:3). In the wake of sin, the curse begins to have a devastating effect upon the creation (3:14, 17; 5:29); yet, even in the post-sin, pre-Abrahamic world, God's blessing abounds (Gen 9:1, 26) and ameliorates the effects of the curse (8:21-22). Blessing belongs primarily to the sphere of creation; it is a gift of God mediated through a human or nonhuman agent that issues in goodness and well-being in life in every sphere, from spiritual to more tangible expressions. As such, all the families of the earth are *not* dependent upon their relationship to Abraham for blessing; it rains on the just and the unjust, and families continue to thrive.[4]

This stands in some tension with the focus on blessing in Gen 12:1-3 and its emphasis in chaps. 12–50 (though 12:2 recognizes that outsiders will mediate blessing to the elect). If God as Creator already blesses the world before Abraham, of what purpose is Abraham's election? The difference following Abraham's election is that blessings will be intensified or made more abundant (see Gen 30:27-30) by this relationship; life thereby will be made even more correspondent to God's intentions for the creation. Israel itself will continue to need special divine blessing all along the way (Num 6:22-27).

God as Lawgiver

The giving of the law is integral to the story of creation, and this is so in two respects. One, human beings are commanded to be fruitful and multiply, to fill the earth, and to subdue it (1:28). Two, they are prohibited from eating of the tree of the knowledge of good and evil (2:16-17). Before sin has entered the world, law is given a prominent place. Even after sin, and before God's choice of Abraham/Israel, law remains an integral part of the created order, as seen in Gen 9:1-7.

By being built into the created order, the point is made that every human being, not simply the chosen people, is to attend to the law for the sake of the creation. Creation entails such law-giving for three basic reasons: (1) Law serves the proper development of God's good creation. The creation is a dynamic reality, always on the move, and law both generates change ("subdue the earth") and gives shape to that unfolding in an ordered way. (2) Law helps order human life to be in tune with the creational order intended by God and, given the link between moral order and cosmic order, such obedience will have a salutary effect on the nonhuman world. (3) Life in creation is not free from all threats; law is given for the sake of the preservation of God's creative work.

When Israel is given the law at Sinai, it is thereby given tasks in the tradition of Genesis 1–2. Israel now stands before God and hears anew the command to have dominion over the earth, to till and keep the land, and to be its brother's keeper (the texts subsequent to Genesis 3 are also revealing of creational commands). The law given at Sinai is not a new reality, but a fuller particularization of how the community can take up its God-given *creational* responsibilities in view of new times and places. By attending to the Sinai laws, Israel grows toward God's intention for human beings that was laid out in the creation. Disobedience complicates these responsibilities immensely, but God's redemptive activity has the effect of reclaiming and enabling true human life, freedom, *and responsibility* within the created order.

God as Judge

The image of God as Judge is also set in place in these chapters. The sin of Adam and Eve (and their descendants) is not treated lightly by God, as if it were a minor matter. The judgment of God, which may be defined as the facilitation of the moral order—seeing that sins do have consequences—plays a key role so that sin and its effects do not have the last word. Hence, God announces the effects of sin on the primary spheres of human life and vocation in 3:14-19, and announces a catastrophic end of all life in 6:5-6, until Noah's finding favor with God ameliorates the range of the catastrophe. At the end of the flood story, God promises never to visit the earth in floodlike ways again; this promise builds into the very structures of the world (hence its canonical placement) a limitation with respect to the effects of human sinfulness. God's judgment will never again be universal in its scope. Wrath(fulness) is not an attribute of God; it is a contingent divine response to a situation in creation (if there were no sin, there would be no wrath). The God who judges is the kind of God confessed in Exod 34:6-7.

But this does not mean that God will not enter into judgment in less thoroughgoing ways. The theme of divine judgment will play a significant role in the rest of the Pentateuch, with respect to both the nonchosen (e.g., Sodom and Gomorrah; the Egyptians) and the chosen (in the wilderness, Numbers 11–25).

God as Relational

Through the lens of these images, the God of the opening chapters of Genesis is seen to be a deeply relational God. Most basically, God is present and active in the world, enters into a relationship of integrity with the world, and both world and God are affected by that interaction. In all of this, God has chosen not to stay aloof, but to get caught up with the creatures in moving toward those divine purposes, and in such a way that God is deeply affected by such engagement. God involves the human in creational tasks; God walks in the garden and engages the human; God ameliorates judgment (4:15); God suffers a broken heart (6:6); God limits the divine options in relating to sin and evil (8:21-22).

The rest of the Pentateuch witnesses to this kind of God. For example, God responds to human prayer, from petition (Genesis 24), to lament (Gen 25:22-23), to intercession (Gen 18:22-33; Exod 32:9-14); in the latter, the divine-human relationship is revealed as having a genuine dialogical character. God even changes the divine mind in view of such interaction (Exod 32:14; see Num 14:19-20). God gives the law, and human beings are to be obedient, but not just because "God said so"; God gives motivations for obedience: the law is given for the sake of life, health, and the flourishing of community. Human beings are to respond to God's gifts, but not as vassals.

These wide-ranging images of God suggest that a primary theme of the Pentateuch will concern God and God's interaction with the world. God is the subject of more verbs than any other character, many of them key verbs: God creates, judges, saves, redeems, elects, promises, blesses, enters into covenant, gives the law, heals, guides and protects in the wilderness, and holds the human party accountable. The kind of God who is active in these ways is succinctly noted in Exod 34:6-7, though that text will take us beyond chaps. 1–11 in its proclamation of God as one who forgives. But these linkages suggest that fundamental to the Pentateuch is the conviction that the God of whom it speaks is a coherent character across its pages. This is not to say that the God of the Pentateuch is absolutely immutable, never changing or "growing," but that such changes are supremely consistent with God's most basic character and universal purpose.

Human Beings as Good and Responsible Creatures

The pervasive and powerful images of God must not be allowed to obscure the high place given to the human in God's creation. Human beings are presented as good and responsible creatures. Created in the image of God, as well as from the dust of the ground, they are given work to do in God's world; they are called to be cocreators with God. They become sinful and this colors everything they say and do, but they remain God's good creation, in the divine image, with the same call to responsibility (3:22-24; 9:1-7). Indeed, faithfulness to God remains a human calling (5:24; 6:8-9).

A variety of texts in the rest of the Pentateuch (from narrative to liturgy to law) are concerned with a vision of what human

51

beings are to be about in the world. God engages them in an enterprise on behalf of the creation, and God will relate to them with integrity (see above). The call to faithfulness will animate these texts, especially the story of Abraham (Gen 15:6; 22). Israel is called to be holy, merciful, and just, as God is (Lev 19:1; Deut 10:12-22); again and again, the text presses concerns of life, health, justice, and community well-being (Deut 30:19). God's own action provides the pattern for human action, and hence the law can never fully define the range and character of human responsibility.

Human Beings as Sinful Creatures

Sin has the effect of breaking down harmonious relationships at multiple levels; it creates divisions between human beings and God, among human beings (men and women; brothers; parents and children), between human beings and the land ("thorns and thistles"), and within the self (shame). It affects adversely the spheres of family and work, of culture and community (4:17-24), of national life (10–11), indeed the larger creational order (the flood). In fact, sin is so deep-seated that "every inclination of the thoughts of their hearts was only evil continually" (6:5); even the flood cannot change that (8:21). Yet, human beings can act against such inclinations (4:7; cf. Deut 30:11-14) and decide for that which is life-giving rather than death-dealing. The narratives that follow pick up on these themes.

One of the more obvious of these effects of sin has to do with familial issues. This is evident in chaps. 1–11 in the emergence of tensions and inequalities between husband and wife (3:12, 16), the envy and violence between brothers (4:1-16), and the disrespect shown to parents by children (9:20-27). Such conflicts mirror a wide range of family conflicts in the narratives that follow, particularly in chaps. 12–50. One need only mention these: Abraham/Sarah/Hagar; Jacob/Esau; Jacob/Leah/Rachel; Jacob/Laban; Joseph and his brothers. Again and again family life is disrupted because of sinfulness rooted deep in the human heart.

To conclude, the opening chapters of Genesis reveal a complex rhetorical strategy with respect to the implied audience (see also the opening paragraphs of this section). These chapters provide a universal frame of reference and reveal a God who is present and active in the larger world beyond Israel and in such a way that the readers—wherever they may be located—can count on such a God for their future. These chapters also bring forth an understanding of humanity that lifts up goodness and responsibility—for the entire creation—in the midst of continuing sinfulness in a way that need not lead either to hubris or despair. No matter the past, God remains committed to the future of the creation. These images set the tone and direction for reading all that follows.

THE SENSE OF AN ENDING[5]

The way in which a story ends is also important for the interpretation of the whole. Indeed, some people read the end of a book first so as to read the whole with a better idea of what the work is trying to do. The ending of the Pentateuch should be considered both in terms of the last chapters of Deuteronomy and Deuteronomy as a whole. Both are important in determining how one reads the Pentateuch. As with the beginning, one seeks to discern the rhetorical strategy employed and how the implied audience might experience such an ending in view of their particular life situation.

A rhetorical approach to the Pentateuch as seen through the book of Deuteronomy highlights the use of hortatory language and its parenetic character (see chapter 7 on Deuteronomy). The book has even been designated "preached law." This use of language makes it clear that it was written to move the reader, to get inside readers and touch not only their minds, but their feelings.

This hortatory character of Deuteronomy ought not be viewed in isolation from the rest of the Pentateuch. It functions as a particular rhetorical strategy for impressing upon the reader the importance of hearing *all* that has preceded. Readers are led through the first four books and brought to this point, where the parenetic language now catches them up in the fundamental import of what God has been about in their lives, with intense and urgent appeals for present response. Indeed, the historical review of chaps. 1–3, as well as later retrospects (e.g., chap. 9), engage the reader once again in key developments that go back through Numbers to Exodus. It may be that earlier hortatory pieces (e.g., Leviticus 26) prepare for this Deuteronomic strategy. The combination of historical retrospects, future possibilities, and the enclosure of the law with the promise (4:31; 30:1-5), while not relaxing the import of faithful response, constitute a wide-ranging appeal to both heart and mind.

Deuteronomy 29–34 may be viewed as the ending of the Pentateuch. These chapters have not commonly been considered a worthy ending of either Deuteronomy or the Pentateuch.[6] This ending has often been regarded as a series of appendixes of mixed genres and interests gathered somewhat haphazardly at the end of the book. Indeed, the ending is not a "normal" one; it does not, say, tie things together into a neat package. But what might it mean that the ending contains so many loose ends? For one thing, it creates a sense of uncertainty regarding the future, and it may reflect the situation of the implied readers, who are at "loose ends" in the face of such a future. This kind of ending leaves readers leaning into the future, but wondering what that future might hold.

A comparable appraisal can be made of the content of the ending. The ending defers the fulfillment of the promise; it gives to the Pentateuch the character of an unfinished symphony. The promise is left suspended and the people are dispirited and fearful (31:6). The future is not simply filled with delights; it is fraught with danger. And the danger comes, not just from the Canaanites, but from the inner recesses of their own hearts (31:20-29).

The considerable body of law in the Pentateuch, even the ending of Deuteronomy (30:11-14), implies that obedience is possible; a community of life and well-being can be created in the land of promise. Human responsibility with respect to life in community is recognized as basic to the shape that the promised future takes. But the same ending also subverts that confidence with repeated drumbeats speaking of Israel's inclination to infidelity and warning of consequent disaster (28:15-68; 29:17-28; 30:17-19; 31:16-29; 32:15-35). The people are called to obey, and indeed they often can, but they are also so deeply inclined to disloyalty that they will not finally be able to control their own future or create the order the law suggests they can. Both law and liturgy will be an ongoing "witness against" their inability to do so (31:19, 21, 26, 28). Deuteronomy leaves readers wondering what might be in store for this inevitably disobedient people. These negative possibilities create an ending of no little ambivalence.

The death of Moses creates an added level of uncertainty. The final verses (34:10-12) briefly recall a glorious past, but it is focused on a person rather than the people; they are a paean of praise for Moses and his great deeds. Indeed, he is made the subject of words most often reserved for God; it is *Moses* who performed "all the mighty deeds and all the terrifying displays of power" (cf. Exod 6:6). Only he has known God "face to face" (v. 10); no prophet in all of Israel's history holds a candle to him. It is true, Joshua is "full of the spirit of wisdom" (34:9), but Joshua is no Moses. Given the loss of Moses, and the propensity of the people to apostasy, this eulogy is not particularly good news for the people. What will they do without Moses and all his mighty deeds (one recalls Exod 32:1-6)? The future does not look so promising. To be left with such an ending is an uneasy, even unnerving experience.

One can observe this disquietude in scholarly assessments of this ending over the last century and more. Because of the nature of this ending, scholars have often been moved to create a different one, and so they speak of a Hexateuch (or "Primary History," or Deuteronomic History [= Dtr], see pp. 58-62). In this way, they get the fulfillment of the promise (of land, at least) as the ending, and the story—to their way of thinking—is appropriately rounded off. In other words, this is a way in which many readers have sought to escape from the unsettling force of the ending.

Yet, the ending does give some basis for hope (29:10-15; 31:1-8; 33:1-29). A genuine sense of expectancy is generated by these texts. But it is qualified by the realism of the human condition, so that the people of God must ground their hope, not in their strength or capacity for obedience, but in the promised presence of God and the certainty of divine faithfulness. It is only because God goes with them and keeps promises that they can be strong and courageous and can be assured that the promises will be fulfilled. And so the basic word at the end of Deuteronomy is "wait on God and hope in God." The way into the promised future is only possible if God is at work, not only in and through this people, but also beyond them and in spite of them.

This sense of an ending, like the Word of God more generally, is a two-edged sword. It lifts up the divine promise as basic to Israel's future, but it also makes clear that human fear in the face of uncertainty and death, a transition in leadership, and an inclination to disobedience endanger participation in that promise.

The ending is rhetorically designed for a community that is in a situation comparable to the original community on the eve of entry into the land of promise.

As such, Deuteronomy's ending is not rhetorically crafted to bring the story to a close; there is a decided open-endedness to the future. But it is still an ending.

THE ENDING MEETS THE BEGINNING

The ending of the Pentateuch has parallels with the beginning, providing brackets for the whole. This doubling constitutes an intensification of these themes for the implied audience. The situation of the first human beings standing before God on the morning of creation corresponds to that of the newly redeemed people of God on the eve of the entry into the land. Just as Adam and Eve are created in the image of God and are commanded to have dominion in God's creation, so also Israel as God's covenant partner is given responsibilities to further the divine purposes for the life and well-being of the creation. In addition, the prohibition given humankind in Gen 2:16-17, the response to which means life or death, parallels Moses' words to Israel about the commandment (Deut 30:11-20).[7]

Both command and prohibition create a "leaning" toward the future; the human response will shape that future into something different from the present. The commands to have dominion and to "subdue the earth" imply that God intends the creation to become something other than what it was at the beginning. Within this purpose, God engages the human, the image of God, as cocreator. But, given the violation of the prohibition, God's intentions for the world, while still focused in life and well-being, have become more complex; God now must work within a situation profoundly affected by sin and its evil effects. Yet, God's engagement of the human as co-creator remains in force (Gen 3:23; 9:1-7; cf. Psalm 8); to that end, the law given at Sinai is a fuller specification of the law given in creation, and that is placed sharply before Israel by Moses (Deut 30:15-20).

The unfaithful response of Adam and Eve to the prohibition resulted in a human condition wherein "every inclination of the thoughts of their hearts was only evil continually" (Gen 6:5; cf. 8:21), and that "inclination" is recognized as being firmly in place at the end (Deut 31:21, 27). This means that Israel makes its choice (Deut 30:19) from within a situation different from that of their first parents and this reality problematizes its move into the future. The stories that follow will be deeply colored thereby. At the same time, Deut 30:6-10 envisions a future for Israel when God will give them a new heart, and obedience and faithfulness will follow naturally (see Jer 31:31-34). Hence, the ending of Deuteronomy takes a significant and unparalleled step beyond Eden.

The move from the judgment of the flood to the postflood promises is parallel to the disasters of Deuteronomy 28 followed by the covenant in chaps. 29–32. Despite the fact that the human heart continues to be inclined to evil, and will result in disasters of one kind or another, God chooses to go with the world and with Israel (Gen 8:21-22; Deut 29–32). Judgment will not be God's final word for either. The promises are made and, given the divine commitment (Deut 4:31; 30:1-6), will remain intact forever.

Finally, the Mosaic era in some sense constitutes a paradigm for each successive generation of the people of God (see Deut 5:3; 29:14-15). God has chosen Israel, delivered them from bondage, constituted them as a people, and come to dwell in their midst. The vision of Leviticus (the center of the Pentateuch), with the people of God encamped around the tabernacle, shaped by their deliverance and given instruction for their life and health as a community, is a pattern for subsequent generations of God's people. Lending support to this understanding are the final verses giving high praise to Moses, who surpasses all the prophets (Deut 34:10-12). The conclusion of the Pentateuch "[designates] . . . the Mosaic age as a constitutive and normative narrative."[8]

At the same time, the book of Numbers (especially), with its recurrent testimony to human sin and failure (and God's response thereto), functions to introduce a sharp note of realism into this picture. These realities will intrude into Israel's life again and again, and the Dtr narrative that follows constitutes ample testimony to this. While the Mosaic paradigm remains in the face of such realities (and may inform images of the reign of David, e.g., 2 Samuel 7; Psalm 72), it does so only as an ideal, something to work and dream toward. The prophets, who are more pessimistic, throw this "dream" onto an eschatological screen (e.g., Jer 31:31-34).

Yet, what future generations of readers seek to do with what they have become by God's gracious action is an issue to be addressed. Even with such a realistic assessment of the human condition, it is recognized that people can make a difference to the world and to God. If this understanding is properly related to the creation story, then both law and liturgy, so prominent in the Pentateuch, are integrally related to this enterprise.

The central role given liturgy (from various festivals to sacrificial acts) lifts up its capacity as a world-making activity; what happens in liturgy is for the sake of the maintenance and the healing of the world (see Leviticus chapter). The issue is not simply Israel as a holy community in itself; the issue is its place, and that of the readers, as a holy community among the nations, for "the whole earth is mine" (Exod 19:5).

DEUTERONOMY AS BEGINNING

While Deuteronomy is an ending, it is also a beginning. Another way to put it: the Pentateuch ends not "with an arrival, but with a suspension of the moment before departure."[9] Deuteronomy both closes one chapter and opens another. Scholars have noted how closely Deuteronomy is linked to the books that follow, in terms of both style and theological perspective. In the present canonical arrangement, Deuteronomy seems to have a double function, closing the Pentateuch and setting the agenda for what follows. In view of this reality, a brief exploration of the latter is in order.

The Pentateuch does not stand alone; it is integrally related to the rest of the Old Testament. Numerous echoes of Pentateuchal themes may be found in the Psalms (e.g., Psalms 78; 105; 106) and the prophets (especially between Deuteronomy and Jeremiah), but its relation to Joshua–Kings is particularly close. The movement from Genesis to Kings constitutes a continuous story from the creation through the origins and development of Israel and the long journey of their life in the promised land, climaxing in the destruction of Jerusalem and exile.

As such, this corpus is sometimes called the "Primary History."[10] The term *Hexateuch* (Pentateuch plus Joshua), commonly used in earlier generations of scholarship, also recognized this link, especially the fulfillment of the land promise. Another designation, the Deuteronomic History (Dtr), is used to refer to Joshua–Judges–Samuel–Kings, because of their links with the literary style and theological perspective of Deuteronomy, which may have originally introduced Dtr. From another angle, scholars have sought to discern Deuteronomic influence in Genesis–Numbers (key texts are Exodus 3–4, 12, 19–24).[11] If correct, this suggests that Genesis–Numbers (sometimes called the Tetrateuch and probably originally separate from Deuteronomy) was editorially integrated with Deuteronomy–Kings at some point.

Among the numerous thematic connections between the Pentateuch and Dtr, the following may be lifted up. They show the extent to which the Pentateuch leans forward into the books that follow and sets their tone, and the degree to which the history of Israel in Dtr "leans back" on this earlier material. In other words, the Pentateuch (especially its Deuteronomic texts) provides a key to the interpretation of Joshua–Kings.

The most commonly observed of these links is the report of the land settlement in the book of Joshua. Joshua 21:43-45 (cf. 1:6; 5:6; 18:3) explicitly and emphatically relates the settlement back to God's promises to Israel's ancestors. The recollective material in Deuteronomy 1–3 focuses on matters relating to the land of promise, and concludes with a ringing statement about what God will do in the future. The people of God need not fear because God goes with them and fights for them (3:21 22).

In Genesis God promised a land to Israel's ancestors (12:7; 15:7-21), a theme picked up in the books that follow (Exod 6:4, 8; Lev 26:42; Num 32:11), especially Deuteronomy (1:8; 6:10; 7:8; 9:5, 27; 29:13; 30:20; 34:4). Even more, Genesis associates this promise with the iniquity of its pre-Israelite inhabitants, the Amorites (15:16, 21; cf. Judg 6:10; 1 Kgs 21:26; 2 Kgs 21:11), a theme also stressed in Deuteronomy (9:4-5; 20:17-18; cf. Exod 34:11-16; Lev 18:24). At the same time, Genesis usually portrays the indigenous peoples of the land in a positive light; indeed, the problematic relationships between Israel and the native peoples are due in part to the sins of Israel's progenitors (e.g., 20:1-18; 34:25-30). In view of the judgment upon Israel's ancestors for the violence perpetrated against these peoples (Gen 49:5-7), the readers are asked to contemplate whether Israel's violence in Joshua is thereby given a mixed evaluation. Was this violence made necessary by the violence of Israel's own ancestors? The net effect is that Genesis understands the land promise as it relates to Canaan's native peoples in ambivalent terms.[12]

It is important to note that, from the perspective of both Pentateuch and Dtr, residence in the land was not necessarily permanent; the Pentateuch anticipates an exile from the land (Lev 26:33-34; Deut 4:26-30; 28:63-64; 29:22-23; 30:18-20), and the loss of land is narrated at the end of Dtr (2 Kgs 25:21). In 2 Kings, Israel is returned to the same position it had at the end of Deuteronomy (even worse, given the partial fulfillment in Num 21:31-32; 32:32), only with the future more uncertain given its apostasy.

The last chapters of Deuteronomy (28–34, plus 4:25-31 and Leviticus 26) have an unusually clear sense of those negative directions Israel's future is likely to take, climaxing with destruction and exile (though the promise remains [4:31; 30:1-5]). Most scholars conclude that these passages were written in light of the actual experience. This seems likely, but, narratively, these chapters give readers a lens through which they are to interpret the books that follow. These negative futures have not been predetermined from the time of Moses; conditional language punctuates these texts (Lev 26:3-27; Deut 28:1-44, 58-68; 30:4, 16-17). Rather, these texts claim that, implicit in the time of Moses, this particular future was a lively possibility (see the "may be" of Deut 29:18).

A few texts, however, make a stronger claim: there *will be* apostasy and judgment (Deut 28:45-57; 31:16-29). "For I know that after my death you will surely act corruptly" (31:29). Such texts ought not be considered predictive; rather, they testify to insight into the sinful human condition and its dire effects ("I know well how rebellious and stubborn you are," 31:27; cf. 31: 21; 9:24). This scenario, however, does not go so far as to say that even if Israel were *obedient,* this would be its future; this future is still "because" they did not obey (28:45, 47). One key function of Deuteronomy is stated in this connection: "as a witness against you" (31:26); the law will reveal Israel's sin for what it is.

The heart of Israel's sin, particularly in Deuteronomy and Dtr, is specified in terms of the first commandment, "You shall love the LORD your God with all your heart, and with all your soul, and with all your might" (Deut 6:5; cf. 5:7; Exod 23:23-33). The first commandment and Israel's response to it become the key to the interpretation of the history of Israel. Both Deut 29:24 and Dtr (1 Kgs 9:8; cf. Jer 9:12-16; 16:10-13; 22:8-9), anticipating the destruction of Jerusalem, ask the question, "Why has the Lord done thus to this land?" The question is answered in terms of the first commandment: "Because they forsook their God . . . and laid hold on other gods, and worshiped and served them." The issue is apostasy, manifested basically in the worship of other gods (cf. 2 Kgs 17:7-18). Being exiled from the land of promise is due, not to a God whose promises have proved unreliable, but to Israel's failure to be faithful to the God who has made the promise.

The problem is thus fundamentally a matter of faith and unfaith and not (dis)obedience of an external code. Failure to keep the commandments is symptomatic of a more pervasive problem, namely, disloyalty to God. To "[reject] *all* the commandments of the LORD their God" (2 Kgs 17:16) finds its definition in terms of unbelief and idolatry (17:14-15). The first commandment is also the focus of "forsaking" the covenant: "because they abandoned the covenant of the LORD, . . . and served other gods, worshiping them" (Deut 29:25-26; cf. 31:16, 20; 17:2-3; Josh 23:16; Judg 2:19-20; 1 Kgs 11:9-11; 2 Kgs 17:15, 35-38). The only "condition" of the covenant is finally faith and trust in God alone.

The ending of Deuteronomy thus sets in place a two-pronged approach to the history of Israel in Dtr, both curse (28:15-68) and yet the continued articulation of the promises of God (30:1-8), both poetically depicted in chaps. 32–33. In the face of Israel's unfaithfulness, the promises continue to be articulated, focused on land and peoplehood. Earlier in the Pentateuch, the golden calf narrative seems designed to show later generations that the ancestral promises still stand in spite of such infidelity (Exod 32:13). And Deut 4:31 and 30:1-10 (cf. Lev. 26:44-45), which have destruction and exile in view, make the strong claim that God "will neither abandon you nor destroy you; he will not forget the covenant with your ancestors that he swore to them," and "from there the LORD your God will gather you, and from there he will bring you back . . . into the land that your ancestors possessed, and you will possess it."

Dtr continues this promissory theme, for example, Judg 2:1, "I will never break my covenant with you" (cf. 1 Sam 12:22), and especially the promises to David (2 Sam 7:16). God's promises will not fail; they will never be made null and void as far as God is concerned. Though a rebellious generation may not live to see the fulfillment of the promise, the promise can be relied on. The promise is an everlasting one, though participation in its fulfillment is not guaranteed to every person or generation. The promise is always there for the believing to cling to, and they can be assured that God will always be at work to fulfill it.

This theme is linked to a certain portrayal of God. The climactic statement about the character of God in the Pentateuch (Exod 34:6-7; Num 14:18-19) stresses the divine mercy and forgiveness available to the sinful community; this theme is also picked up in Deuteronomy (4:31; cf. 7:8-9; 10:15-18) and Dtr (1 Kgs 8:15-53; cf. 2 Sam 22:51; 24:14; 1 Kgs 3:6; 10:9; 2 Kgs 13:23). God is revealed as one who has proved faithful to promises given to the ancestors, though the people often have proved faithless. God is revealed as a patient God, not bound to some retributionary scheme, but "moved to pity" time and again (Judg 2:18), giving Israel another chance to repent of their unfaithfulness (2 Kgs 13:23). And even, finally, when disaster must fall, it is cast in terms of death, but not annihilation, for judgment is perceived as a refining fire, as a means by which life might finally come again (Lev 26:44-45; Deut 4:25-31; 30:1-10). No word of final rejection is ever announced.

CONCLUSION

This chapter has sought to show that the strategic placement of certain claims regarding God and the divine-human relationship has been designed to shape one's reading of the entire Pentateuch. It is now more evident that the Pentateuch as a whole is fashioned to shape the faith and life of its readers. More specifically, as will become clear in the Deuteronomy chapter especially, this strategy serves an end having to do not so much with the *fides quae* (the content of the faith), but with the *fides qua* (the faith itself).

Hence, the most basic effect desired for readers is not that they become better theologians or better informed about their history and traditions. The end desired is more deeply religious, namely, that the relationship with God become what God intended in the creation. The theology of the Pentateuch is an applied theology; indeed, it may be said that its theology is in the service of proclamation. All that God has done on behalf of Israel is given in such rich detail "so that you and your children and your children's children may fear the LORD your God all the days of your life, and keep all his decrees and his commandments . . . so that your days may be long" (Deut 6:2) and, finally, so that God's "name [may] resound through all the earth" (Exod 9:16).

In part 2, each of the five books of the Pentateuch will be approached from the viewpoint provided by this rhetorical strategy. Each chapter will be developed somewhat differently, taking into account the distinctive structural and thematic features of each book, as well as its prominence in the history of interpretation.

PART TWO

THEMES AND STRATEGIES IN THE PENTATEUCH

CHAPTER 3

THE BOOK OF GENESIS

NATURE AND ORIGIN

Genesis is a book about beginnings. It moves from the morning of the world to the ordering of families and nations to the birthing of the fathers and mothers of Israel. While God was there "in the beginning," Genesis also testifies to the beginnings of God's activity in the world. It is a new day for God, too. And, given the divine commitment to the creation, God will never be the same again.

But creation is more than chronology. Genesis stands at the beginning because creation is such a basic theological category for all that follows. All of creation, from the least to the greatest, is shaped daily in decisive ways by the life-giving, life-enhancing work of the Creator. Creation provides the matrix within which God acts; creatures are born, mature, and die; and the divine-creature relationship develops. Only in relationship to creation can God's actions in and through Israel be seen to be universal in scope. God's work in choosing and redeeming Israel serves creation, the *entire* creation; God thereby reclaims a universe that labors under the pervasive effects of sin. God's initially exclusive move is in the interests of a maximally inclusive end—a new creation.

Genesis consists of two primary types of literature, narratives and genealogies, into which various poetic pieces have been integrated (e.g., 49:1-27).

1. Ten genealogies constitute major portions of seven chapters of Genesis, providing its most basic structure: 2:4 (heaven and earth); 5:1 (Adam); 6:9 (Noah); 10:1 (Noah's sons); 11:10 (Shem); 11:27 (Terah); 25:12 (Ishmael); 25:19 (Isaac); 36:1, 9 (Esau); 37:2 (Jacob). These Priestly genealogies are supplemented by others (e.g., Cain [4:17-26]). One type of genealogy is linear (one person in each generation [5:1-32]); the other is segmented (multiple lines of descent, characteristic of nonchosen lines, such as Esau). Genealogies usually introduce a section, but at times they look both forward and backward (2:4; 37:2).

The historical value of the genealogies is debated, but families and tribes no doubt relied upon them to track family "pedigrees" for social or political purposes. More generally they show that every person—chosen and nonchosen—is kin to every other; even more, in view of 2:4, human and nonhuman are linked together in one large extended family. Theologically, genealogies stress God's ongoing creational activity of bringing new lives into being and ordering them into families. While they witness to order and stability, narrative pieces within their flow (e.g., 5:24, 29; 10:8-12; cf. 4:17-26) introduce elements of disequilibrium and unpredictability.

2. The form of the narratives is difficult to assess. They are not historical narrative in any modern sense, though they do possess features associated with history writing (e.g., cumulative character and chronological framework). The primary concerns of these texts are theological and kerygmatic, written by persons of faith in order to speak a word of/about God to other persons of faith. As such, Genesis is not socially or historically disinterested; it was written—at each stage of transmission—with the problems and possibilities of a particular audience in view (see chapter 2).

The designation "story" (or story of the past) is perhaps most helpful in determining how these materials functioned. The stories are told in such a way that they could become the stories of each generation; at the juncture of past story and present reality, Israelites came to know what it meant to be the people of God. By and large, the world reflected in these stories is ordinary and familiar, filled with the surprises and joys, the sufferings and the troubles, the complexities and ambiguities known to every community. At the same time, Genesis is God's story. These stories disclose a world in which God has become deeply engaged, not to bring people into heavenly spheres, but to enable a transformation of life in this world. This admixture of the human story and God's story provides for much of the drama that these stories present.

Scholarly efforts to reconstruct the history that lies behind chaps. 12–50 have had mixed results. A period of some confidence in the basic historicity of this material within the second millennium BCE has faded in recent years. Putative ancient Near Eastern parallels to ancestral names and customs have at times been overdrawn. Yet, they are not finally without historical value, even for a second millennium dating at some points. It seems reasonable to claim that the narratives carry some authentic memories of Israel's pre-Exodus heritage. One such matter pertains to the religious practices reflected in these texts, which are often distinctive when compared to those of later Israel. This would include the worship of God under various forms of the name El (see 16:13; 21:33; 33:20; El is the high god in the Canaanite pantheon) and reference to God as God of my/our/your father (31:5, 29, 42).

Genesis is a composite work with respect to the origins of the literature (see chapter 1), but in time it has been shaped into a unified composition. This can be seen in the relationship of the beginning and the end of the book. Genesis moves from a "good" creation to the "good" that God works in Joseph's family (50:20); from family disruption to brotherly reconciliation; and from the seven days of creation to the seventy descendants of Jacob entering the land of Egypt. Joseph functions as a new Adam (e.g., 41:38), for not only the Egyptians, but the entire world benefits from his "dominion" (41:56-57), and the command to be fruitful and multiply is fulfilled in this family (47:27). At the same time, no new Eden emerges; sin and its effects remain deeply embedded in human hearts and social structures.

Leading themes that cross the traditional division between

chaps. 1–11 and 12–50 underscore the book's unity. We have marked several in chapter 2: God is one who creates, promises, blesses, elects, saves, and judges. Creational themes are also common, much more so than generally recognized: the presence and activity of God in every sphere of life; the role of the human as both sinner and cocreator with God; the concern for the non-human world; the pervasive interest in kinship and family; attention to issues of economics, agriculture, and the dynamics of political and governmental life. The range of interest in Genesis is breathtaking.

Certain developments over the course of the book may be noted. In literary terms, the narratives move from episodic vignettes, tied together by itineraries or genealogies, to more sustained narratives with clearer plotlines. Theologically, God's words and deeds become less direct and obtrusive. While God is never all-controlling, a more prominent role is given to the human along the way, climaxing in the Joseph narrative. Human life becomes more complex as the family of Abraham and Sarah moves from occasional interactions with outsiders to a place on the world stage.[1]

THE PRIMEVAL STORY (1:1–11:26)

The last century has seen a proliferation of new directions in the study of these chapters: comparative studies based on the discovery of Near Eastern creation and flood accounts; new literary approaches, historiographical methods, theological developments; and issues generated by scientific research, environmentalism, and feminism. We have learned truths about the origins, development, and nature of the world of which the biblical authors never dreamed.[2]

These realities have sharply complicated the interpretation of these chapters: How old is the earth? Does Genesis 1 commend the exploitation of the earth? Are these texts inimical to the status of women in church and society? In seeking to address such issues responsibly we must go beyond the text and draw on insights from other parts of Scripture and from our own experience in and through which God continues to speak. Yet, these chapters will continue to provide the modern reader with an indispensable foundation for such reflections, including the images of God and the human, the relationships between God and the world, and human and nonhuman interrelationships.

Israel was not the only people in the ancient Near East with stories of creation; indeed, one example, the Babylonian epic *Atrahasis* (1600 BCE), contains a creation-disruption-flood sequence. It is apparent that Israel participated in a culture with a lively interest in these questions. Israel drew on a widespread fund of creational images and ideas in shaping its own accounts, but was probably not directly dependent on written texts. These ideas from the larger world were genuine contributions to Israel's reflections on creation, while important differences were maintained: the absence of a theogony and a conflict among the gods, the lack of interest in primeval chaos, the prevailing monotheism, and the high value given human beings.

Determination of the type(s) of literature present in chaps. 1–11 is difficult. While they often mirror human life in every age, the past and the present are not simply collapsed into each another. These texts do purport to tell a story of the past, though they are not historical in any modern sense ("history-like" is a term sometimes used). This concern for the beginnings of things is evident in the atypical aspects of some texts (e.g., the long-lived patriarchs belong to an irretrievable past, as does the reality of one language [11:1]) and in the interest in genealogy and chronology (e.g., 8:13-14). On the other hand, the typical may be reflected in the use of the word *'adam*, which refers to generic humankind (1:26-27), the first man (2:7), or Adam (4:25). The typical and the atypical have been interwoven in these texts. For example, Genesis 2–3 speaks both of a past, subsequent to the creation, when sin and its evil effects emerged into the life of the world *and* of a typical encounter with the reality of temptation.[3]

The structure of these chapters is shaped by the interweaving of genealogy and narrative. The narratives move in parallel panels: (a) from beginnings (1:1–2:25) to sinful individuals (3:1-24) through family (4:1-26) out into the larger world (6:1–8:19), ending in catastrophe; (b) another beginning (8:21–9:17), moving again through sinful individuals and family (9:18-27) out into the world (10:1–11:9), only this time into a world that Israel clearly knows. The genealogy of Shem (11:10-26) also provides an individual point of reference that reaches out through the family of Abraham into the larger world (12:3*b*).[4]

The thematic direction of these chapters has been worked through in chapter 2, but might be summarized here. The recurrent litany that God has created everything good stands as a beacon regarding the nature of God's creative work and God's intentions for the creation. The *subsequent* entrance of sin, while not finally effacing the God-human relationship or the key role human beings play in the divine economy, has occasioned deep and pervasive ill effects upon all relationships (human-God; human-human at individual, familial, and national levels; human-nonhuman) and dramatically portrays the need for a reclamation of creation. On the far side of the flood, God rejects annihilation as the means to accomplish this reformation and graciously chooses a more vulnerable, long-term engagement, working from within the very life of the world itself. The world continues to live and breathe because God makes a gracious, unconditional commitment to stay with the world, come what may in the wake of human sinfulness.

At the same time, not every concern in these chapters should be collapsed into a theological mold. Genesis 1, in particular, provides considerable evidence of what we would call scientific reflection. Israelites were interested in the "how" of creation, and not just questions of "who" and "why." So, available data about the natural world was integrated with theological perspectives. This move recognized that both spheres of knowledge must be used to understand the world. Readers in every age are implicitly invited to do the same, to take whatever additional (at times contradictory) knowledge has become available over the years (e.g., some form of evolution) and integrate it with theological and confessional statements.

The Creation and Disruption of the Universe (1:1–6:4)

1. *Two Creation Stories Become One* (1:1–2:25). Many think that Genesis 1–2 consists of two creation accounts, assigning 1:1–2:4a to the Priestly writer and 2:4b–25 to the Yahwist (see source criticism discussion in chapter 1). Differences in literary type, structure, vocabulary, style, and center of concern have been noted. Yet, while the two accounts have different origins and transmission histories, they have been brought together in a theologically sophisticated fashion to function *together* as the canonical picture of creation. In the following paragraphs I seek to read them as such.

Signaled by the shift in 2:4 from "heaven and earth" to "earth and heaven," chap. 2 focuses on the earthly context; it may be intended to describe in detail several days of chap. 1, especially the sixth day. In this linkage, diversity and complexity in the imaging of creation are valued more than strict coherence. God is characterized as one who creates *(bara')* and makes *('asah)*, who speaks and separates, who forms and builds from existing material, and who engages that which is already created in the creational process (see 1:11; 2:19). Analogies from human creating are common, and the verb *bara'*—God is the only subject and it carries no object of material or means—may be used to affirm that no such analogy adequately portrays God's creative activity. Although ordering (of material depicted in v. 2 usually) is the primary effect of this divine activity, the diverse images, the less than perfect symmetry (e.g., eight creative acts in six days), and the call to the human to "subdue" the earth, convey a sense that this creative order is not forever fixed. The creation is presented as basically in place, but still in the process of becoming. Hence, appeals to the "orders of creation" (on, say, ethical issues) must be handled with considerable care.

The opening verses of chap. 1 are difficult to translate and hence interpretations will vary. The most convincing (and common) position is to translate v. 1 as an independent sentence and to interpret it as a summary of the chapter (as with the genealogies in 5:1; 6:9; 10:1; and 11:10); v. 2 describes a state of affairs prior to God's ordering, a state that is not *yet* consonant with the divine purposes in creation; v. 3 reports the first creative act. The "chaos" of v. 2 refers not to some divine opponent (unlike Babylonian parallels), but to raw material that God uses to create what follows, when it ceases to exist.[5] The author does not deny that God created all things, but the origin of what is depicted in v. 2 is of no apparent interest.

The word "beginning" thus is not the absolute beginning of all things, but the beginning of the ordered creation, including both spatial and temporal orders. The seven-day order (climaxing in the sabbath, 2:1-3) establishes a temporal pattern to be observed by all human beings, so that life will be in tune with the creative order. This concern for a work-rest weekly rhythm makes it likely that the days of creation are to be understood as twenty-four-hour periods; this is early "prescientific" reflection, and moderns must consider perspectives from scientific disciplines to discern a fuller truth about the origins of the world.

The basic content of the eight act-six day structure is ordered in terms of parallels between spaces and their inhabitants: days 1 and 4 (light/luminaries), days 2 and 5 (waters/firmament; fish/birds), days 3 and 6 (dry land/vegetation; land/animals/people/food). Among the repetitive phrases associated with these creative acts, "God saw that it was good" is especially noteworthy. Here God reacts to the work, making evaluations; 2:18 ("it is *not* good") implies that such evaluation was part of an ongoing process for God, within which change is possible. The subdue language of 1:28 implies that "good" does not mean perfect or static or in no need of development, but appropriate for God's intended purposes. The divine naming (1:5-10) stops with the earth's appearance, and human beings pick up that task in 2:19. For both, naming denotes not authority (so Adam's naming of Eve does not entail subordination), but a discernment of the creatures' place within the creation.

Although the creation of humans does not require an entire day, a change in language signals the importance of their creation. The "let us" language (1:26) images God as a consultant of other divine beings; the creation of humankind results from a dialogical act, an inner-divine communication. This language reveals the richness and complexity of the divine realm. God is not in heaven alone, but is engaged in a relationship of mutuality and chooses to share the creative process with others. Human beings are created in the image of one who creates in a way that shares power with others. While the meaning of the image of God is open to much debate, it refers basically to those characteristics of human beings that make communication with God possible and enable them to take up the God-given responsibilities specified in these verses (this image remains intact after the entrance of sin [9:6]). That human beings, like other creatures, are also created from the dust of the earth (2:7) constitutes the other pole regarding human identity.

The image functions to mirror God to the world, to be as God would be to the nonhuman, an extension of God's own dominion. This text democratizes an ancient Near Eastern royal image so that all interhuman hierarchical understandings are set aside. That both male and female are so created means that the female images the divine as much as the male; likeness to God pertains not only to what they have in common but also to what remains distinctive (providing a basis for the use of female images for God, e.g., Isa 42:14; 66:13). The command to have dominion, in which God delegates responsibility in a power-sharing relationship with humans, must be understood in terms of caregiving, not exploitation (see Ps 72:8-14; Ezek 34:1-4). The verb "subdue" has reference to the earth and its cultivation and, more generally, to the becoming of the world. This indispensable role for the human is also lifted up in 2:5 and 2:15, where a pre-creation state remains because there was as yet no human being to serve ("till") and keep the ground.

With this divinely ordained role, male and female, in turn, are placed in a garden in Eden (thought to be in the Jordan valley [13:10?]). God is imaged as a potter in designing and creating the first human being (a male figure rather than an earth creature, as some have suggested[6]); God's very life is breathed into him. God places two trees in this garden; they are associated with life and death and human choices related thereto (see Deut 30:15-20). The tree of life is a means of continuing life, but from which God bars the man and woman after they have eaten of the tree of knowledge (3:22). The tree of the knowledge of good and evil, a knowledge that God has (3:22), presents a use of the law wherein certain creaturely limits are recognized as in the best interests of human well-being. These limits are associated with a divine knowing, by which humans are to acknowledge the decisiveness of the Word of God for true human life; they anticipate the giving of the law at Sinai. To conceive of these matters in terms of an eating metaphor, so prominent in Genesis 2–3, signifies taking something into the self that shapes one's total being ("you are what you eat"). The penalty for eating is death—capital punishment, not mortality—for death as such is part of God's created order (otherwise the tree of life would have been irrelevant).

In 2:18 God identifies a problem with the creation at this point—human aloneness—and moves to resolve it. That God first brings animals to the man shows that the issue being addressed is companionship, not sexuality or procreation. That "helper" does not entail subordination is likely in view of its common use for God (Ps 121:1-2). That God gives such an important decision to the man—"whatever," without qualification (2:19)—shows the extent to which God delegates power, engages the human in the creative process (cf. 1:11), and leaves room for human decisions that truly count in the shaping of the future. Such a commitment on God's part involves risk, since human beings may (and in time do) misuse the power they have been given.

Given the human decision, God brings to the man a personally designed and constructed woman—made from living flesh (probably "rib" rather than "side"). Being created from a part of the man does not entail subordination any more than man's being created from the ground does. The man recognizes that the woman addresses the stated need, and his exultation counts for a "good" evaluation. His words (v. 23) stress mutuality and equality, with a new level of knowledge of his identity as a man in relationship to a woman. The concluding verses do not mention children, but focus on the man-woman relationship; they are now "one flesh," which refers to intimacy in the broadest sense of the term, not just sexual.

The garden has sometimes been described in overly romantic terms, for the text shows much restraint (ancient Near Eastern parallels are minor). Genesis emphasizes the basics: life, freedom, food, a home, a family, harmonious relationships, and a stable natural environment. The contrast with the situation in 3:7-19 is clear, if at times overdrawn, and to that we now turn.

These various images regarding creation are certainly important for the implied audience, so much in need of God's creative activity in the midst of the collapse of their ordered world. These chapters would thus parallel the use of creational themes on the part of key prophets (Isaiah 40–55; Jeremiah 31–33).

2. *The Intrusion of Sin and Its Social and Cosmic Effects* (3:1–6:4). Genesis 3 has played an extraordinary role in the history of interpretation, if not within the Old Testament itself (Ezek 28:11-19 has some connections). It probably did not gain this status until post–Old Testament times (e.g., Rom 5:12-21). But care must be used not to overdraw this point. The text's placement at the head of the canon gives it a certain theological stature.

At the same time, chap. 3 does not stand isolated, and its larger context should play a more important role than it commonly has. While the literary and thematic links with chap. 2 are often noted, less attention has been given to the chapters that follow. For example, similarities in the outlines of chap. 3 and 4:7-16 should keep these texts closely connected. This link should be extended through 6:1-4, where the cosmic effects of sin are mythically conveyed, with 6:5 summarizing the situation at that juncture: "every inclination of the thoughts of their hearts was only evil continually." No such claim is made at the end of chap. 3, though that has been a common interpretation. Rather, chap. 3 describes the "originating sin," and the chapters that follow speak of a process by which sin became "original," that is, universal and inescapable. When this processive understanding is combined with the primary imagery of separation, estrangement, alienation, progressively greater distances from Eden, and the decreasing ages of human beings, "fall" language is reductionistic and not entirely appropriate for chap. 3.

No word for "sin" occurs in chap. 3; it first appears in 4:7, where it is given an enticing, possessive character. This absence has made it difficult to agree on the nature of the primal sin; what do the human beings do that is wrong? A closer look at some details of the story will assist readers with such a question.

Chapter 3 brings readers into the middle of a conversation between a snake and two human beings (3:6 makes clear that the man is present the whole time). Is the snake a malevolent or demonic creature, out to seduce humans away from God? Not likely. The snake is identified as an animal of the field, as in 2:19-20 and in God's sentence (3:14). The humans seem to so understand the snake; they express no fear or wonderment, perhaps because animals in the garden are given capacities of thought and speech (cf. Job 12:7-9). The snake is an ambivalent symbol, associated with both life and death (see Num 21:4-9), and also with craftiness (cf. "sly fox"), perhaps because of its ability to sneak up on others. The verbal link (in Hebrew) between the naked humans and the snake's craftiness suggests that human beings may be *exposed* at times to shrewd elements in God's world, language appropriate for temptation. So, the snake presents a metaphor, representing anything in God's good creation that could present options to human beings, the choice of which would seduce them away from God. The snake facilitates the options the tree presents. As is common, the facilitator participates in the consequences of the choice and the metaphor is established as a negative one for the future (3:14-15).

The reader overhears the conversation at the point it evolves into a question about God and the prohibition. The snake asks questions that carry the conversation along, and responds in ways that are truthful: the humans do become like God, knowing good and evil (3:22), and they do not die, at least physically; in fact, they could eat of the tree of life and continue to live. The key phrase that leads to the eating is "God knows" (3:5). It highlights the fact that God has not told them the full truth. And the question is thereby raised as to whether God, having kept something from them, indeed something that seems beneficial, could be fully trusted with their best interests. The issue of knowledge at its deepest level is an issue of *trust*. Can the humans trust God while pursuing the truth about God? Trust that God has their best interests at heart even if they do not know everything? Trust that not all "benefits" are for their good? The primal sin may thus best be defined as mistrust of God and God's word, which then manifests itself in disobedience and other behaviors.

The serpent has presented possibilities through words (only) and the humans draw their own conclusion.[7] Rather than speak to God about the issue, they silently consider the tree and the wisdom it offers. The issue is not the gaining of wisdom, however, but the way it is gained ("the fear of the LORD is the beginning of wisdom" [Ps 111:10]). What this entails can be seen from the result. Only God can view the creation as a whole; the humans do not have such a perspective, nor the wherewithal to handle their new knowledge very well. The woman takes of the fruit and—with no tempting words—gives it to her silently observing partner. Even now, he raises no questions and considers no religious issues; he simply and silently takes his turn. The man and woman are in this together.

Their eyes are opened, that is, they see each other and the world differently, entirely through their own eyes; left to their own resources they are indeed naked, though not literally so. Their human resources—loincloths—prove inadequate, as they hide from God (3:10). Their clothing reveals more than it conceals (as does God's clothing the already clothed in v. 21). In 3:8-13, the man is the primary subject, balancing the female subject of vv. 1-7. The Creator of the universe—no aloof God this—does not leave the humans or walk elsewhere. God seeks a response from the fearful and ashamed human beings, but they move to the "blame game" rather than confession. The sin has led to dissonance in interhuman relationships, between humans and God, between human and nonhuman, and within the self (e.g., shame).

Most would say that 3:14-19 are descriptive (of what happens in the wake of sin) rather than prescriptive (divinely established orders for the future). Yet, the language of divine judgment is appropriate if understood as God's announcement of what the sinful deeds (including those in vv. 8-13) have wrought. Human beings reap the consequences of their own deeds in terms of their primary roles in that culture. Every aspect of human life is touched: marriage and sexuality; work and food; birth and death. It is especially remarkable that the "rule" of the man over the woman is seen as a consequence of sin rather than God's creational intention.[8] More generally, human beings wanted control over their own lives; they now have control in grievously distorted and unevenly distributed forms. They wanted to transcend creaturely limits, but they have found newly intensified forms of limitation. They now have the autonomy they desired, but not the perspective to handle it well.

But this state of affairs has not been put in place for all time to come; no new orders of creation are established. Indeed, as with any consequences of sin, effort should be made to relieve the toil, pain, patriarchy, and negative effects on nature ("thorns and thistles"). Such endeavors harmonize with God's intentions in creation, though continuing sinfulness impedes the effort. Even in the wake of these effects, God remains in relationship with the creatures, and hopeful signs for the future emerge, though expulsion from the garden becomes necessary. The naming of Eve anticipates that life will go on; God acts to cover their shame with more substantial clothing; even exclusion from the possibility of never-ending life could be interpreted as gracious given what they had become. The humans leave the garden with integrity, still charged with caring for the earth. While being "like God" severely complicates life, it also bears some potential for good and advancement. The expulsion mirrors later Israelite banishments from the land because of disloyalty to God (see Leviticus 26).

The effect of these garden events on family life now follow. The story of the world's first children in chap. 4 presupposes a more densely populated world (Cain's wife; building of a city; concern for his life). Yet, the text may belong with those (e.g., 2:24) that collapse the distance between the "then" of the story and the "now" of the reader. The story portrays how the effects of sin cross generations, afflict even families (a basic order of creation), and lead to intensified levels of violence (cf. 6:11-13). The story also sets in place key themes for the rest of Genesis: family conflict, primogeniture (God's not choosing the elder son), sibling rivalry, and divine promises given to the nonchosen (e.g., Ishmael, Esau).

The story begins positively with responses to God's commands to be fruitful and multiply (Eve), to have dominion over the animals (Abel), and to subdue the earth (Cain). The initial focus on worship as integral to creation sees the brothers bringing appropriate offerings. God, however, rejects Cain's offering, for reasons unknown; Cain's dejected response to God's choice is not the problem so much as his interaction with God about it. God makes clear that Cain is able to master his anger, but Cain kills Abel anyway. God, having been called by the blood of one unable to seek justice, calls Cain to account for the murder. When Cain deflects the question, God more intensively applies to Cain the earlier curse on the ground (3:17), the banishment, and the distancing from God's presence. When Cain objects to what amounts to a death sentence, God mercifully ameliorates the sentence by promising (!) to be Abel's brother's keeper and sealing the promise with a mark (its nature is uncertain). Ironically, the restless wanderer proceeds to build a city. Such an image once again mirrors the experience of an implied audience in exile.

The genealogies portray two different family lines (Cain, 4:17-26; Seth, 5:1-32) that flow from this conflicted family. Both positive and negative effects are portrayed. A powerful rhythm within life that works for good persists: intimacy that brings new life into being, creative advances in the arts of civilization, the invoking of the name of Yahweh (by those who were not Israelites!), people who walk with God such as Enoch. Yet, violence becomes more intense (Lamech), and the diminishing age spans may depict the effects of sin (though also characteristic of other Near Eastern lists of long-lived patriarchs). Progress in civilization is accompanied by progress in sin and its effects.

The effect of these realities on the cosmic sphere follows in 6:1-4, and continues into the flood story. This difficult text, with its depiction of the crossing of boundaries between the heavenly and earthly realms, may portray the cosmic effects of sin, with new possibilities for violence. This would, then, be a natural lead into the flood story, in which the entire cosmos is caught up in the effects of violence and is threatened with extinction.

The Flood: The Great Divide (6:5–8:22)

This text is usually recognized as an interweaving of J and P stories (see the discussion of source criticism in chapter 1). That Israel would have preserved more than one version of the flood is not surprising since flood stories circulated widely in that world, of which the one in the *Gilgamesh* epic is the most well known. The basis for these stories is probably a severe flood in the Tigris-Euphrates valley (such a flood occurred ca. 3000 BCE), which in time was interpreted as a flood that covered the then-known world.

The focus of the present text is signaled by the repeated conviction about human sinfulness (6:5; 8:21) and the associated disclosures regarding divine sorrow, regret, disappointment, mercy, and promise. God appears, not as an angry judge, but as a grieving and pained parent, distressed at developments; yet, the judgment announced is thorough and uncompromising. This inner-divine tension is resolved on the side of mercy when God freely chooses Noah (6:8). Noah's faithful walk with God, exemplified by his obedience (6:22; 7:5, 9, 16; 8:18), becomes a vehicle for God's new possibilities for the creation.

The flow of the story leads up to and falls away from God's remembrance of Noah and the animals in 8:1. The story itself gives repeated attention to the boarding of the ark, to lists of people and animals/birds that are saved, to what God does to bring salvation rather than judgment, and to the chronology of the event. Remarkably little notice is given to the disaster itself, to the plight of its victims, and to the feelings of the participants; no dialogue is reported and Noah does not speak. The flood is described in natural terms—"what goes around comes around"—with no divine act of intervention; only with the subsiding of the waters is God's explicit activity stated.

The ecological themes in the text are significant. Humans have a deeply adverse impact on the creation; thorns and thistles (3:18) grow to cosmic proportions and the world's future is endangered. God's assigning temporal limits to the flood (7:4) assures that the orders of creation will not break down completely, and God's remembrance of the animals and birds (6:19; 8:1) belongs to the same initiative as God's remembering Noah.

Scholars have proposed overlapping interpretations of the flood: cleansing (yet 8:21 speaks of human sinfulness); undoing creation in order to begin again (yet major continuities with the original creation remain); judgment as typical divine response (yet the flood is unique, for God promises never to repeat it); a polemic against other flood stories (yet, in spite of many differences, Israel learns from such materials). More likely, the interpretive key lies in the view of God presented and the divine commitments made to the flood's survivors. The images of God are striking: a God who expresses sorrow and regret; judges reluctantly; goes beyond justice and determines to save some (including animals); commits to the future of a less than perfect world; is open to change in view of experience with the world; and promises never to destroy the earth with a flood again. It is precisely this *kind* of God with whom the implied audience, still at sea, deals, and it is primarily the divine commitment to promises made that it needs most to hear.

A New World Order (9:1–11:26)

The postflood account of the Priestly writer (9:1-17) picks up the theme struck in 8:21-22: God now speaks directly regarding the changed relationship to a still sinful world. This world is no new Eden, but every creature—human and nonhuman—is assured that God is still the Creator and that the basic divine relationship to the world still holds, with its blessings and (adjusted) commands.

The dominion charge is complicated in view of the "fear and dread" of human violence, the human diet is supplemented with meat as a concession in a famine-ridden world (a theme in 12–50), and the proscription regarding blood (see Lev 17:11) stands as a sharp reminder that killing animals must not be taken lightly, for God is the source of their life. Moreover, the high value of human life is affirmed; an understanding of the human as image of God still pertains in the postflood world. The lifeblood of human beings is not to be shed, much less eaten. Indeed, murderers are directly accountable to God for their actions. At the same time, human life is not absolutely inviolable; humans can forfeit their right to life if they take a life.

God makes a covenant (9:8-17), a promise publicly stating the divine commitment of 8:21-22 to those who have endured the flood. The repetition of words and phrases emphasizes the promissory character of the covenant—never again!—and the inclusiveness of its recipients through all generations, which would include the implied audience (see Isa 54:9-10). This unilateral and unconditional covenant is an obligation that God assumes; it will be as good as God is, and so human beings can rest back in its promises. The sign of the rainbow serves *God's* remembering, that is, action with respect to a prior commitment (see Exod 2:24), but it becomes a secondary sign for people in which they can take comfort and hope. This divine restraint in dealing with evil is an eternal limitation of God's exercise of power; it sets the direction for a different approach to the redemption of the world, beginning with Abraham.

The remaining segments in chaps. 1–11 serve several purposes in preparing for God's choice of Abraham. (1) They bring the reader into a world whose peoples and places reflect known historical realities. Even a kind of secularity is introduced, for God does not speak or act in 9:18-27. (2) They extend human relationships beyond the family into the world of nations, where problems and possibilities of various sorts take on a communal aspect. (3) It becomes clear that the flood has not cleansed the world of sin and the curse; the new Adam (Noah) and his sons get caught up in their spiraling effects. The theme of dysfunctional families continues and sets the stage for the rest of Genesis. (4) Goodness persists alongside human failure. The blessings of God's creation continue to abound in the proliferation of families, the development of civilization, and the appearance of the family of Shem. Abraham emerges from within this family and this kind of world, and it is for the world's sake that he is called, so that "all the families of the earth shall be blessed" (12:3).

The first text (9:18-29) contains difficulties that cannot be pursued here. One key is that Noah's sons are presented both as individuals and as ethnic units (for example, the Canaanites), as in chap. 10. God's postflood blessing begins to take effect amid the world of the curse, ameliorating its effects, for example, the vineyard and its wine, which symbolize God's blessings of life and fertility (see Ps 80:8-16). At the same time, human sin (drunkenness and parental disrespect of some sort, perhaps the public disgrace of the father) and intrafamilial conflict abound, leading to communal difficulties—including slavery—among the descendants (9:25-27).

The second text (10:1-32), the table of nations, delineates all the known peoples of the world eponymously, that is, in terms of their descendance from Noah's three sons. Such multiplying and ordering of the peoples into an international community is witness to God's continuing creational work. Problems of identification remain, but basically the horizon of the list extends from Crete and Libya in the west to Iran in the east, from Arabia and Ethiopia in the south to Asia Minor and Armenia in the north (the world known to the implied reader). The recurrent use of the word "families" links this chapter to 12:3.

The third text (11:1-9), centered on the city/tower of Babel, seems out of place after the table of nations, where people are already scattered (10:18) and Babel is named (10:10). But the two sections are not in chronological order; 11:1-9 reaches back and complements chap. 10 from a negative perspective. Links with the implied audience may be present in the scattering of the people from the city—note the typicality of the "whole earth" reference. The central human failure in this text is not easy to discern, but seems focused in the motivation, "otherwise we shall be scattered abroad upon the face of the whole earth" (11:4). Only because of this does building a tower and making a name become problematic, namely, an attempt to secure their future isolated from the rest of the world. This constitutes a challenge to the divine command to fill the earth (1:28; 9:1) and fulfill the charge to have dominion; human concern for self-preservation places the rest of the creation at risk. God counters these efforts by acting in such a way—by confusing languages—that they have no choice but to scatter and establish separate linguistic communities. God thereby promotes diversity at the expense of any kind of unity that seeks to preserve itself in isolation from the rest of the creation.

From one of these scattered families, Abraham is raised up for God's mission with respect to all such families.

THE STORY OF ABRAHAM (11:27–25:18)

Our approach to the rest of Genesis will take a somewhat different form from that taken to chaps. 1–11. An overview will be provided for each of the major cycles (Abraham, Jacob, Joseph),[9] followed by an overarching survey of key themes.

84

The book of Genesis, which has had the world as a stage, now narrows down to a small town in Mesopotamia, to a single family, to the mind and heart of an individual—Abraham. At the same time, the world stage remains very much in view. Abraham is deeply rooted in that world's culture, remains in touch with people from various nations, and is called by God to mediate blessing to its families (12:3). Moreover, God is not narrowly associated with Abraham's family but remains engaged with this larger world. So, while chaps. 12–50 will now focus on the progenitors of Israel, the links with the universal interests of chaps. 1–11 are deep and broad.

Other links across this divide might be noted. In chapter 2 we pointed up continuities in the imaging of God and human beings. God remains active as one who creates, blesses, elects, promises, gives the law, judges, saves, and is deeply engaged in relationship with the creation. Regarding human life, the downward spiral that began in Eden and plunged the world into cosmic catastrophe still pertains. For the family of Terah (11:27-32) it means early death, infertility, and interrupted journeys. Difficulties and tragedies, sinfulness and evil will pervade Abraham's story, too. God does not return the world to its original form nor does God perfect people before choosing to work through them, as will soon become evident. Yet, the genealogies testify that life, however troubled, continues, and God's promise to Noah ensures the world's future.

So, this shift to Abraham does not mean a new world or a new divine objective for it. God's post-sin objective of reclaiming the world so that it reflects the divine intention remains in place. But we now have a clearer view of the *divine strategy* for moving toward this goal. The story does not say why God chose Abraham and his family rather than another, but it does make clear that God chose them for the purpose of reclaiming the creation. The election of this family is to serve the mission of God.

The Abraham story is somewhat episodic in character—more so than the stories of Jacob and especially Joseph will be—and it is difficult to discern how everything coheres. Source criticism (see chapter 1) has dealt with this reality by identifying distinctive strands of tradition (J, E, and P); but, whatever one might say about the complex history of this material, it has now been decisively shaped by a narrative flow and themes that encompass the entire cycle.

Numerous efforts have been made to discern the structure of the narratives. The promise of land centers the first part of the story (12–15), while the promise of a son centers the last part (15–22), with chap. 15 inverting the two (vv. 1-6; 7-21). The most obvious of its structures is the doubling of key stories over the course of the narrative[10]: genealogies, which enclose the story (11:10-32; 25:1-18); references to the "old country" (11:27-32; 24); the endangering of Sarah (12:10-20; 20:1-18); Lot (13–14; 18:16–19:38); Hagar and Ishmael (16; 21:8-21); the birth of Isaac (18:1-15; 21:1-7); Abimelech (20; 21:22-34); a testing of Abraham in association with a journey (12:1-9; 22:1-19). Most scholars find the center of the story in the doubling of the chapters focused on covenant (15; 17). These doublings give to the narrative an ongoing mirroring effect, inviting another look at Abraham and the development of God's purposes in and through him over the course of his journey.

THE STORY OF JACOB (25:19–36:43)

Jacob is Israel; this claim informs and animates these chapters. Jacob remains a person in his own right, but over the course of the story he *becomes* Israel, so that finally he is more than an individual. Over the course of many centuries Israelites told and retold the stories of Jacob; in that process the inherited stories and the ongoing experiences of Israel were interwoven. The result is that these texts tell both a story of the past and a story of all who go by the name of Israel. The portrayal of this progenitor of all Israelites is remarkably realistic and unpretentious. Jacob appears with qualities that are negative and positive, clear and ambiguous, simple and complex. Take him or leave him. The most astounding claim is that God takes him.

The cycle is introduced as the story of Isaac (25:19), but the reader quickly discovers that it centers on his sons, Jacob and Esau. In fact, the story of Isaac himself is reduced to an interlude (26). As with Abraham, the stories of Jacob occur in somewhat episodic form, tied together by itineraries or genealogies, yet chaps. 30–31 provide a more sustained narrative of Jacob's stay with the kin in Haran and the story's plot makes for more internal cohesion. So, the story evidences both compositeness (J, E, and P) and unity.

86

A journey provides the broad cohesiveness of the story: Jacob's flight from Canaan to Haran and back to Canaan. Genealogies of Ishmael and Esau (25:12-18; 36:1-43) bracket the narrative, and keep relationships with nonchosen peoples clearly in view. The center of the story, with an explosion of God language, is the birth of the progenitors of most of Israel's tribal groups (29:31–30:24). Their birth within the matrix of the Jacob-Laban conflict, as well as the many associated hardships, may reveal Israel's self-understanding. Israel's birth was difficult indeed and, born in the midst of conflict, the story mirrors much of its later life.

The four appearances of God constitute the "pillars" of the story and provide for its key developments. God's oracle to Rebekah regarding the future of the "wrestling" twins in her womb (25:23) sets the agenda for much that follows. God's appearances to Jacob at Bethel, before he leaves the land (28:10-22) and after his return (35:9-15), with their interest in the divine promises, provide continuity for Jacob across the divide of his sojourn in the "far country." Finally, Jacob's wrestling with God at the Jabbok (32:22-32) sets a God-Jacob conflict alongside the Esau-Jacob conflict, and reveals a God who becomes deeply engaged *within* Jacob's conflictual relationships.

JOSEPH, JUDAH, AND JACOB'S FAMILY (37:1–50:26)

Although these chapters focus on Joseph, 37:2 announces that this is "the story of the family of Jacob." The reader must think fundamentally in corporate terms; the concern is the emergence of Israel's family as Israel, the people of God. This prepares the way for the subject of the book of Exodus, as it moves the family from Canaan to Egypt and introduces that setting, especially the court of Pharaoh. While the story continues themes from the prior narrative (e.g., promise and family conflict), it extends them by integrating family history with national and political history.[11]

Source critical approaches have regarded the story as a composite work (J, E, P, and redactors), a view prompted by so-called doublets, and the seemingly intrusive nature of chaps. 38 and (portions of) 46–50. Yet, chaps. 38 and 46–50 are more coherent if one understands this to be a story of the emergence of the tribal groups of Israel more than that of an individual. In any case, this story is less episodic than those of Abraham and Jacob. It may even be desig-

nated a short story or novella, with a plot moving from crisis to resolution (similar to Ruth and Esther).

As for its origins, scholars have often pointed to the influence of
the wisdom movement on the book, for example, the portrayal of
Joseph as an ideal administrator. Along with other themes, this
could point to a royal setting, and the Solomonic era has been suggested. At the least, concern is evident regarding the proper ways
in which leadership is to be exercised.

As for structure, the story follows the genealogy of Esau; its
announcement that Esau is Edom (36:1) is now followed by a comparable move from individual Israel to people Israel. The story
itself begins with a conflicted family situation, and two brothers
seem to be eliminated from the line of promise (37–38); it ends
with the resolution of conflict and the inclusion of all of the brothers within the orbit of promise (50). Chapters 39–44 develop along
two lines—the Egyptian context and Joseph's rise to power
(39–41) and family interrelationships (42–44), with an initial climax in the meeting of the brothers in chap. 45. Each of these
developments in its own way makes possible the emergence of the
people of God in chaps. 46–50.

NARRATIVE THEMES

The following discussion highlights four prominent themes in
the ancestral stories—journey, creation, God's promises, and
human faithfulness. I consider each of these themes in turn while
attending to the flow of the narrative in Genesis 12–50.

Journey

Journey is a basic metaphor in the ancestral story. It functions
at the literal level, but it must not be left at that. The journey signals something basic about the life of faith and the interaction
with God and other human beings. It also mirrors the life of Israel
during much of its history, not least that of the implied audience.

God begins the story by calling Abraham to a pilgrimage (12:1-
3); Abraham's faithful response moves him, not only to Canaan
but through it, all the way to Egypt and back again (12:4–13:4).
The story culminates with journeys, as Abraham again heeds
God's command and travels with Isaac to the mount of sacrifice
(22), followed by the journey of Abraham's servant to find a wife

for Isaac (24). In between there are several journeys (14; 20), but this metaphor also functions at another level as we observe how Abraham's faith works itself out in interaction with God and outsiders.

The story of Jacob is also centered by journeys. He is forced to leave Canaan because of familial conflict, encounters God on the way (28), and travels to the family home in Haran, where he spends years in "exile" as a kind of journeyman (29–31). Heeding God's call to return home, the journey takes him through encounters with God (32) and Esau (33); the story concludes with Jacob journeying through the land of promise (35). Again, we are given a close look at how a person of faith functions when confronted with a range of adversities and how he develops in response, and how encounters with God give decisive shape to this development.

The story of Joseph is set in motion by the journey—eventually to Egypt—forced on him by his brothers (37). As the story unfolds, numerous journeys back and forth between Canaan and Egypt are undertaken by Jacob's family. The story in Genesis ends with this family settled in "exile" in Egypt, and the rest of the Pentateuch will follow them on a complex journey out of Egypt, through the wilderness, and back home.

Hence, Genesis 12–50 is about individuals and a family on the go, often forced by conflict and external pressures to move, but never far from engagement with God. These individuals' journeys both within and without the promised land mirror the life of later Israel with all of its conflict, especially exodus, land settlement, and exile. They connect in special ways with the experiences of the implied audience, who have been through a major conflict and are exiled from the land of promise. At the same time, the tortuous travels of this family are joined by God, whose presence and punctuating promises provide direction and hope. Yet, though the journey reaches out toward a promised future, it always comes up short of final fulfillment. The "better country" of which Hebrews speaks (11:16) will remain stretched out before people of faith until their dying day.

Creation

We noted above how the universal interests of chaps. 1–11 remain in place in chaps. 12–50. The reader should be alert to the importance of this theme for the implied audience, exiled in a foreign land, in constant contact with outsiders, questioning God's relationship to such folk, as well as their own, and wondering about God's continued involvement in their lives given the recent experience of destruction and dispersion. That these stories surface in the exilic prophets (e.g., Isa 51:2) is significant.

1. *God.* The call of Abraham does not narrow God's channel of activity down to a history of salvation. God remains active in every sphere of life, among outsiders as well as insiders. Moving through the cycle, one sees God concerned about blessing all the earth's families (12:3); engaged in Egypt and within its royal house (12:10-20); in conflicts with ancient empires (14:20); in the ministrations of the king-priest, Melchizedek (14:19); in the life of the Egyptian slave, Hagar, and her son Ishmael, for whom God exhibits deep care, to whom God speaks five (!) promises (16:7-13; 17:20; 21:13-19), and of whom it is said, "God was with the boy" (21:20); in the judgment upon Sodom and Gomorrah and in the engagement with Abraham over its fate (18:16–19:29); and in the life and dreams of the Canaanite Abimelech (20). Note, too, the divine blessing implicit in the genealogies of Ishmael and his half-brothers (25:1-18). Among such outsiders, God is present; and among them God judges, defeats, and destroys, but also blesses, communicates, cares for, promises, heals, uses as instruments, saves, and embraces within the divine purposes for the world.

These outsiders, in turn, respond in ways that are theologically sophisticated and their behaviors often put the chosen family to shame. We encounter Melchizedek, who mediates the blessing of Abraham's God (14); Hagar, the only person in the Bible who, in view of her experience with God, gives God a new name (16:13); Abimelech, who exemplifies a fear of God in a way that Abraham does not and who calls Abraham to account for his deeds and serves as his confessor (20) and offers a theological interpretation of events (21:22-23; 26:28-29); and relatives, who know and trust Abraham's God (24:31, 50-51), as is also the case with Abraham's servant, whose prayers are exemplary (24:42-49).

Moving to the story of Jacob, God is less frequently the subject of verbs, and there is less material about outsiders, except, of course, Esau, the progenitor of Israel's Edomite neighbors. God remains related to Esau, though in ways less specific than with Ishmael (the blessing evident in his wealth [33:9; 36:7], and his genealogy). Indeed, Esau never mentions God and God does not act or speak directly relative to him after 25:23, though Jacob does see the "face of God" in Esau's reception of him (33:10). Also, Abimelech again interprets God's activity (26:28-29), and the relatives in Haran—Arameans—continue a God-fearing stance. Laban, trickster though he is, so gives witness (31:49-50, 53), and God speaks to him (31:29, cf. 30:27).

The Joseph story depicts the Creator God in ways somewhat different from chaps. 12–36. Although not mentioned less often (some fifty times), God acts in less direct ways. God does not offer oracles (God never appears to Joseph) and miracles; rather, God weaves the threads of goodness, mercy, and judgment into the texture of ordinary life, both private and public, working toward the best possible end. Joseph associates with no centers of worship and builds no altars. Yet God is with him, blessing him at every turn, and he is imbued with God's spirit (41:38).

In the story of Joseph, the primary outsiders in view are the Egyptians. That God is engaged for good within the land of Egypt is apparent not least in the way in which Egypt prospers under the leadership of Joseph. Indeed, a ruler of Egypt acknowledges that Joseph's success is due to the presence of the Lord in his undertakings (39:3). Generally, the Egyptians treat the chosen family in such a way that their lives are preserved and they are able to develop as a community (47:27); they even deeply grieve the passing of Jacob (50:7-11). Given this basically positive portrayal of the Egyptians, readers will have difficulty demonizing them when they come to the book of Exodus. God has been at work among the *Egyptians* for good.

2. *The Human Community.* One aspect of God's creative activity is ordering the world into communities: families, tribes, and nations. In these texts, one thinks especially of issues relating to kinship and family. Chapters 12–50 have been called "family narratives" and no real parallels exist in the rest of the Old Testament. Much attention is given to matters such as birth (especially complications); love (24:67) and marriage (e.g., issues of endogamy/exogamy [24:1-67]); parenthood (e.g., identity and age [17:15-19]); and family death and burial (23:1-20; note even the concern about who attends Abraham's funeral [25:9]!). The genealogies, which bracket the Abraham story (11:27-30; 25:1-19), are concerned with familial relationships, as are texts about

inheritance (15:2; 21:10). In the Jacob story, these family interests continue (the births of children [25:21-26 and 29:31–30:24 are especially prominent]). This is somewhat less the case in the Joseph story, not least because it reaches beyond the familial sphere into another order of God's good creation, the world of nations.

Another way of looking at this matter is through the lens of family systems theory. Abraham's family is dysfunctional, and family conflicts in chaps. 4 and 9 have shown the way. Note the following: the wife/sister issues between Abraham and Sarah (12:10-20; 20); the "strife" between Abraham and Lot over land (13); the triangulated relationship among Sarah and Hagar and Abraham (16–18, 21); Lot and his family (19); perhaps even Abraham and Isaac (22).

The Jacob and Joseph stories are also replete with family conflict, which generates their basic plots. In the Abraham/Sarah stories the conflict is centered between the parents; in the stories of Isaac, Jacob, and Joseph the focus is on the conflict among sons/brothers. At the same time, this conflict often spills over into the lives of parents, wives, more extended family members (e.g., Laban), the neighbors (Abimelech; Shechem), and even God (32:22-32). The vital and usually positive role that women—especially Rebekah, Leah, Rachel, and Dinah—play in these conflicts has only recently received significant attention.[12]

It is important not to reduce these conflicts to a sociological or psychological phenomenon. A key to these stories is that *God's choosing, speaking, and acting* generates much of the conflict. For example, God's oracle to Rebekah (25:23) stands at the beginning of the Jacob story and this divine decision to elect one person rather than another occasions deep rifts within the family. But this divine decision does not mean that the future is determined. The way in which the characters respond (e.g., 25:29-34) is important for the direction of subsequent developments. The principals are to respond faithfully and how they work through the divine choices and promises shapes the future (26:3-5), including God's.

The Joseph story integrates family history into other orders of God's creation—nation and government. This story values a good relationship between family and government, embodied in Joseph, who is both brother and national leader. Government should function like a healthy family system. It takes wise governmental figures—such as Joseph—to enable nations to provide the social and economic order needed for the well-being of the citizens.

God works through families and nations in pursuance of the divine purposes, centered on preserving and enhancing the lives of people. God, not human heroes, provides the unity in these stories. Yet, God's work does not remain independent of the healthy functioning of families and nations, and individuals will have a lot to say about that. Indeed, the important role of the human in the divine economy is lifted up again and again, and is not set aside by God because of human failure. But there will be failures and the misuse of power, and these texts reveal how troubles, as well as blessings, will accompany the human journey. Again and again, God will have to work through the pervasive levels of sin and evil to bring about good.

3. *The Chosen Family.* Abraham's family frequently encounters outsiders: Egyptians (Pharaoh, 12:10-20; Hagar, 16:1; 21:9); other empires, including pre-Israelite rulers of Jerusalem (14); Sodom and Gomorrah (18–19); Canaanites (20; 21:22-34); Hittites (23); and Arameans (24). Note also the interest in the progenitors of the Moabites and Ammonites (19:37-38) and the Ishmaelites and other Arabian tribes (25:1-18). This interest is certainly related to the call to be a blessing to such families (12:2-3). How well this call is fulfilled may be discerned in the various ways the chosen relate to these peoples. Both positive (Abraham interceding for Sodom and Gomorrah [18:23-33]) and negative (Abraham endangering Abimelech and his family [20]) models are developed.

God's choice of Jacob rather than Esau (25:23) to continue the line of promise propels this story forward, and the linkage of this family with all the families of the earth is reiterated, especially as its dispersion throughout that world is contemplated (28:14)— this language connects well with the situation of the implied audience. Jacob's contacts with outsiders are more limited than Abraham's (cf. relationships with Canaanites in chaps. 26; 34), not least because the story is preoccupied with Jacob's relationship to Esau, the progenitor of Israel's Edomite neighbors. Their conflict, grounded in God's word and shaped by parental preferences (25:21-28), has a mixed character; each can be faulted for behaviors toward the other as they compete for the blessing. In the end, they settle in their own territories, both with ample blessings, but their relationship is finally deeply ambiguous, and probably deceptive (33:14-17). The other outsiders in the story are the Arameans, the family in Haran. Despite the conflict, both sides recognize that Jacob's presence among them has indeed mediated blessing (30:27-30), and they somewhat warily conclude a covenant of peace (31:51-52).

In the story of Joseph, the Egyptians are the chief outsiders. The contributions of Joseph to their well-being are considerable. Blessings come to these people through his political acumen and economic savvy (39:5; 41:46-49); indeed, the entire world comes into view, as all peoples receive benefits from his wisdom (41:53-57). It should not have been difficult for the implied audience, immersed in a sea of outsiders in exile, to have drawn conclusions about how their relationships with outsiders should be tied to this ancient mission of God. At the least, as Jer 29:7 would advise, the exiles were to "seek the welfare of the city where I have sent you into exile, and pray to the LORD on its behalf."

4. *The "Natural" World.* The reader is confronted immediately with the barrenness of Sarah (11:30; it is not necessarily a physical problem); it remains a key theme throughout, resolved only when Isaac is born, near the end of the cycle (21:1-7). To this might be related the barrenness of the wife and female slaves of Abimelech (20:17-18; cf. the plagues in 12:17), and the healing that Abraham's intercession makes possible. This theme continues in the Jacob story, as both Rebekah and Rachel (25:21; 30:1) have difficulty conceiving.

Another natural feature concerns ecological matters, focused on the land. The promises of God include land (12:7), which is fought over within the family (13) and without (14; 21:22-34). Yet, this gift of God is often subject to famines (12:10; 26:1; 42:5; 47:13). The divine blessing has a precarious character; the land can become something other than what it was created to be, and not consistently sustain its inhabitants. The land Lot chooses—where Sodom and Gomorrah are located—is described in paradisaic terms, but the reader is notified that it will experience an ecological disaster (13:10), which is realized in 19:24-29 (cf. its peculiar makeup [14:10]). This move from Eden to ecological nightmare is grounded in human behaviors (18:20-21); cosmic order is linked to moral order, a reality moderns can readily understand. The same claim is not made for the famines, but Israel does so in other texts (see Deut 11:13-17; 28:22-24).

How directly God relates to these disasters is difficult to discern. One approach speaks of judgment as other than an explicit divine decision. God's judgment does not introduce something new into a situation; rather, God facilitates the moral order, that is, tends to the orders of creation, which function in such a way that the consequence corresponds to the deed ("what goes around comes around"). Anticreational deeds will have negative creational effects (cf. the plagues in Exodus).

An implied exilic audience would be reminded of military siege, which included devastating effects upon the environment (cf. Jer 4:23-26; Isaiah 24). And the prophetic view of the future would include a kind of environmental cleanup, a re-creation of the wilderness (Isa 35:1-10). Generally, these broader creational understandings provide the necessary grounding for considering God's more specific ways of being present and acting within the community of faith, to which we now turn.

God's Promises

Promise stands at the beginning of Israel's ancestral story (12:1-3); it creates Abraham's faith and generates the basic shape of his life. God's promises are decisive for the future of this family and, through it, all the world's families. Having given promises, God is committed to them, and so the future changes for God as well. Promises also stand at the climax of the story (22:16-18) and are repeated at key junctures (12, 13, 15, 17–18, 24). Alongside promises to the chosen stand promises to Hagar/Ishmael (16–17, 21) and Abimelech (20:7). That God makes promises to the nonchosen (cf. 9:8-17) provides an important link between insider and outsider in their experience of God.

Because of Abraham's faithfulness with respect to his son (22:16-18), the remaining promises are transmitted directly by God to Isaac (26:3-5, 24) and to Jacob (28:13-14; 35:11-12; 46:3-4). God's promises are both familial and individualized for each person (see 28:15). God does not speak the promises to Joseph or his brothers; this task is given over to the human community. Jacob transmits the promises to Joseph (48:3-4, 21) and Joseph passes them on to *all* the brothers (50:24); no brother is singled out. The major promises made by God are of a son; of land; of nation, name, kings, and descendants; of blessing; and of presence.[13]

1. *A Son.* The promise of a son was enhanced over the years by the other promises just mentioned. This process extends the promises beyond Abraham's lifetime (he saw only the promise of a son fulfilled) to an open future. Initially, it is not clear whether the mother of the son will be Hagar or Sarah; only in 17:16-20 does God make the promise to Sarah, and in terms that make her parallel with Abraham. It appeared that Ishmael would be *the* son (16:15-16); then Isaac comes into view, but even he does not appear as fulfilled promise until Abraham's fidelity is tested in chap. 22. Chapter 24 reinforces the sonship of Isaac.

Chapter 22 is climactic.[14] This "test" of Abraham, but not known as such by him, is intended to test his faithfulness (so that God may know [v. 12]), not to kill Isaac. It is especially poignant in that he has just lost his son Ishmael; now the "only son" left is endangered. These stories are mirrors of each other, focusing on the potential loss of both sons, and God's provision for both. Abraham's silent response seems cruel (and child abuse questions are close at hand), but it may be that the *reader,* informed by Abraham's challenge of God in 18:23-25, is to respond with questions this time. While God's command (in view of the promise) is bizarre, Abraham's response is informed more and more (over the course of the journey) by a conviction that God can be trusted finally to save Isaac (which places the burden back on God). This surfaces in the key vv. 7-8 (cf. v. 5), where Abraham conveys this confidence in his attentive response to Isaac's question. Isaac's response shows he believes his father's trust is well placed. The provision of a ram for the sacrifice (which was God's intention from the beginning), and God's overriding of the original command with another, confirm Abraham's trust.

This story presents a metaphor for Israel's life with God, in which the implied audience may see itself in both Abraham and Isaac: God has put Israel to a test in the fires of judgment in which many children died, has called forth its continuing faith, has delivered it through the judgment, and renewed the promises. Out of this traumatic experience Israel developed an understanding that a sacrifice was necessary to assure Israel's future, seen most profoundly in Isaiah 53 (cf. 53:7 with Gen 22:7-8). Israel's redemption would not occur without cost.

2. *Land.* The promise of a land (12:7) provides the initial focus for the story, with a choice of lands given to Lot (13), the threat provided by surrounding empires and the links to Jerusalem (14), and the sealing of this promise in covenant (15:7-21). This theme is reinforced at the end of the story of Abraham in the purchase of a burial site in the land (23).

Abraham's family did not experience the fulfillment of this promise. For them and for every generation, these promises continue to play a role *as promises;* they give direction to life and a shape to one's hopes and dreams. So, promises are crucial for the life of faith apart from specific fulfillments, though sufficient experience of fulfillment (first son, then descendants, then land) seems important for continuity in the community's hopes.

3. *Nation, Name, Kings, and Descendants.* These promises are stated at various points, to both Sarah (17:10) and Abraham (17:3-6). The first three promises are fulfilled in the Davidic empire. As for descendants, fulfillment is more complicated; it is interpreted in both a literal and spiritual sense. Literally, it centers on Isaac (for fulfillment see Gen 47:27; Exod 1:7), but it also includes descendants through the lines of Hagar/Ishmael and the children by Keturah—Arabian peoples (25:1-6). The New Testament draws on this fulfillment in the genealogy of Jesus (Matt 1:1), but extends the "offspring" of Abraham spiritually to include all those who "belong to Christ" (Gal 3:29; 6:16). The legacy of Abraham includes not only Jews and Christians, but the adherents of Islam, who track their descendance through Hagar and Ishmael (the Koran has many references to the Abrahamic tradition). That this is basically a spiritual heritage is seen in the fact that 85 percent of Muslims are not of Arabian descent. Does this Islamic reality not mean that God has been faithful to promises made to Hagar/Ishmael? That these three religions hold the Abrahamic tradition in common should assist the adherents of these faiths in their continuing conversations.

4. *Blessing.* This promise is given a central place by virtue of its place in the call of Abraham (12:1-3) and its common appearance throughout chaps. 12–50. Blessing is a gift of God (mediated through human or nonhuman agents) that issues in life and well-being within every sphere of existence. It becomes a catchall word, encompassing the promises noted above, as well as creational realities such as life and fertility, which all of God's crea-

tures experience independent of their knowledge of God. Within creation, blessing is life-enabling and life-sustaining, but it is finally insufficient for the fullest possible life. And so, the *specific promise* of blessing brings focus and intensity to God's activity in and through the chosen family that finally has redemption in view. It is this special blessing that constitutes the bone of contention between Jacob and Esau (27). As noted, the mediation of blessing to outsiders highlights chaps. 12–50.

One of the more remarkable narratives in the Jacob cycle is the story of God's wrestling with Jacob and blessing him (32:22-33). As a fearful and vulnerable Jacob is about to reenter Canaan and confront his brother, God struggles with him for an entire night. This encounter anticipates and shapes Jacob's final encounter with Esau. The most unusual, even stunning feature of this story has to do with God—that God would engage Jacob physically, and then not prevail. God here appears in human form (see 16:7) to encounter Jacob with a comparable power (one ought not think that God could have pinned Jacob at any moment God chose). As for Jacob, he is not passive or submissive; he holds his own with God and, even when struck, retains the power to grant God's request for a release (though daylight would mean death upon seeing God). Yet, God retains the power to grant Jacob the blessing he desperately wants. God breaks the impasse by making the first move: blessing Jacob and giving him the name Israel, which is interpreted to mean that Jacob has prevailed in his struggles with God and humans. The blessing seals the prior promises (28:15) at just the point where Jacob's life is most in danger; God binds himself to go with Jacob into future struggles. In the struggle with Esau, Jacob sees in him, not an enemy, but "the face of God" (33:10). Overall, this story may be viewed as a God-initiated exercise in human becoming—shaping and sharpening the faithfulness of human beings for the challenges to be faced; and God promises to be at the side of those going through such struggles. This is an important word for the implied audience.

5. *Presence.* The promise of blessing to Abraham (12:2) and to Sarah (17:16) implies an ongoing presence of God in their lives, as does the new formulation in 17:7-8, "I will . . . be God to you and to your offspring after you." But the explicit promise of presence awaits God's word to Isaac, "I will be with you" (26:3, 24); it is passed on to Jacob at Bethel in a word of individualized care

(28:15), and repeated for his trip into Egypt (46:4), where God himself goes with him into "exile." God's promise of presence with Jacob during two forced journeys outside the land (which Jacob confesses has occurred [31:5, 42; 35:3; 48:15]) is no doubt a hopeful word for the implied audience.

It is not clear why these promises are arranged as they are, but to have them so regularly punctuate the narrative helps keep the reader's mind focused on them. This would have been important for the implied audience, so tempted to despair (cf. Isa 49:14). It is striking that the promises—land, nationhood, name, descendants, presence—are so attuned to a group of exiles and their future as a people. That descendants are mentioned thirteen times in chap. 17 alone would not be missed by such folk. They, too, would be living short of fulfillment; but promises generate hope in God's possibilities. The key would be their trust in the God who keeps promises.

Human Faithfulness

The story of Isaac exhibits the import of Abraham's faithfulness (26:3-5, 24). Texts highlighting his trust in God enclose the cycle (12; 22), as Abraham launches out on journeys for which the ending is not clear. A key text in the central covenant section—Abraham "believed the LORD; and the LORD reckoned it to him as righteousness" (15:6)—becomes paradigmatic for what the New Testament means by faith (Romans 4; Galatians 3–4). The future is shaped not simply by the God who promises, but by the way in which recipients respond (see 22:15-18). Abraham is not passive, as if the drama were shaped solely by God's will and word. Indeed, his initiatives (e.g., questioning God about Sodom and Gomorrah) and those of others (e.g., Sarah's efforts to give Abraham a child through Hagar) are not signs of a lack of faith; they illustrate the depth of God's engagement with, and commitment to, human beings as the instruments of the divine purpose (cf. 1:28).

Jacob's faithfulness is less exemplary than Abraham's perhaps, but it also mirrors the lives of most persons of faith. It is tempting to so lift up the shortcomings of Jacob—what a cheat and rascal he is—that the signs of his faithfulness are difficult to discern. But Jacob is, perhaps above all, a person who exemplifies his faith by holding God to God's promises. This is evident in the way in which he receives those promises (28:20-22), how he prays (32:9-12), and above all by the way in which he wrestles with God, refusing to let go (32:22-33). In addition, the faithfulness of women in the story should be highlighted. Rebekah enters into the lives of her sons in ways that she believes will contribute toward the future of which God has spoken (27); she is even open to death on behalf of the God whom she serves (27:13). Leah and Rachel, each in her own way, bear witness to the God who has given them children (29:31–30:24) and take active roles in the furtherance of God's purposes in this situation (31:16, 33-35).

The faithfulness of Joseph shows itself in still another way. Joseph's leadership in and through governmental structures is exemplary. Joseph is no passive member of the community, but rather becomes deeply engaged on behalf of the public good. He rejects violence and revenge and brings closure to the snowballing effects of familial dysfunctionality. While Joseph's methods may be questioned—one thinks of the discomfort caused his father and brothers—he finally does not respond in kind, though it is in his power to do so. The one who has ample reason to retaliate chooses the way of reconciliation.

Human beings can neither preserve nor annul God's promises, for God will keep promises; but their words and deeds will have much to say in how those promises move toward fulfillment. Human beings—in whatever situation, even in exile—make a difference to God and to the shape the future takes.

CHAPTER 4

The Book of
Exodus

NATURE AND ORIGIN

Our approach to the book of Exodus will proceed along several lines of inquiry. After some historical comments, we will consider the book's narrative flow, the structures presented, and some leading themes through the lens of a key text, namely Exod 19:3-6.[1]

The book of Exodus has long been a special resource for those who wish to study the beginnings of Israel as the people of God. This study has centered in the narratives concerning the Passover, the Red Sea crossing, and the giving of the law at Mt. Sinai. These events were constitutive for the people of Israel and they have continued to be recognized as foundational for ongoing communities of faith.

Regarding sources, Exodus is a patchwork quilt of traditions from various periods in Israel's life. The epic traditions (J and E) are significantly represented in chaps. 1–24 and 32–34 and carry the basic flow of the narrative. Priestly traditions (P) are interwoven throughout these chapters, but are concentrated in chaps. 25–31 and 35–40, where matters relating to the sanctuary and the priesthood are laid out in great detail.

While the book of Exodus purports to tell a story of Israel's past, efforts to reconstruct the history of this period have proved very difficult; generally, the results of such scholarly endeavor are that Exodus contains a very mixed set of materials from a historiographical perspective. The narrative does not help the historian by, for example, omitting the names of the pharaohs, a fact that suggests that historical concerns are not of primary interest. Some consensus exists that representatives of Israel's later ancestors lived in Egypt for a time, as did other Semitic foreigners during the second millennium. Some linguistic influence is evident in, for example, Moses' Egyptian name. Construction activity by certain pharaohs in which slave labor was employed, particularly in the fourteenth and thirteenth centuries BCE, lends a certain plausibility to the Egyptian oppression. For most scholars this has suggested an early thirteenth century BCE date for the exodus. Yet the times and places of the exodus and wilderness wanderings are quite uncertain, occasioning much debate. It is probable that stories of a number of movements by various tribal groups have been integrated to form a single narrative. So, while a nucleus of these texts is probably rooted in events of this period, the narratives also reflect the degree of significance that thoughtful Israelites, over the course of many centuries, assigned to their past.

The material in Exodus is remarkably diverse in both form and content. With respect to form, the two primary genres of the book are narrative and law. The interweaving of these two types of literature is one of the chief characteristics of the book (for further reflection, see the chapters on Leviticus and Numbers). The interweaving of narrative and liturgical material is also common in Exodus; the most important examples of this feature are the Passover and festival of unleavened bread texts in chaps. 12–13 and the sea crossing texts in chaps. 14–15, which climax in the Song of the Sea in 15:1-21 (for fuller comment on these and other structural characteristics in the book of Exodus, see below). With respect to content, the narrative follows Israel on a journey of immense consequence, to which we now turn.

NARRATIVE FLOW

The book of Exodus begins with a series of vignettes that set the stage for the remainder of the book. God's creational and historical promises are fulfilled among Jacob's family in Egypt (1:1-7). But this resolution is threatened by genocidal forces embodied in an oppressive Pharaonic regime (1:8-14). Initially, God works behind the scenes in and through the wisdom and courage of five lowly women (1:15–2:10); the actions of Pharaoh's daughter toward Moses anticipate those of God toward Israel. The creative disobedience of these women preserves a future for Israel and enables the emergence of a leader in the person of Moses, whose first actions against oppressors (2:11-22) anticipate those of God.

An intensification of God's activity (2:23-25) issues in the commissioning of Moses and an extensive dialogue wherein Moses voices eight objections to God's calling, interrupted by an initial confrontation with Pharaoh that fails (3:1–7:7). This is followed by a series of plagues (7:8–11:10) that become increasingly a threat to Egypt's well-being. The plagues may be viewed as the effects of Pharaoh's genocidal policies. His sins violate the integrity of God's creation and have cosmic effects; violations of the moral order have an adverse effect upon the natural order in virtually every respect (see Hos 4:1-3). The plagues are not an arbitrarily chosen divine response (note also the human agency [11:10]); God gives Pharaoh up to reap the natural consequences of his behaviors (the hardening of his heart being one). The effects are cosmic, because the sins are creational. We have here a picture of creation gone berserk, breaking the bounds of its createdness, reverting to a state of chaos in response to such human behavior.

Although common parlance refers to these events as plagues, the narrative uses the language of sign and wonder (7:3); as such, they are ecological signs of historical disasters (Passover, the Red Sea crossing). God's activity against Egypt must thus be placed on a cosmic screen; God acts for the sake of the entire creation. The public character of these events is important in this regard, expressed in one way in 9:16—so that God's name may be declared on all the earth. The stylized form of the plague accounts may reflect a ritual that dramatized an experience of ecological disaster.

The effect on Pharaoh personally is reported in the references to the hardening of his heart (or will). Both God and Pharaoh (or his heart) are the subjects of three hardening verbs that occur twenty times. That both are subjects is important, as is the sequence. In the course of the plagues, God first becomes the subject at the sixth plague (9:12). Pharaoh's own obduracy is the prior reality; his stubbornness is *intensified* by God's action. His pattern of willfulness in time becomes irreversible through continual refusal to respond to God's word; more and more the end becomes a certain matter (Pharaoh is last the subject in 9:35, the seventh plague), but that was not determined from the beginning (God's statement in 7:3 notwithstanding).[2]

Moses announces the tenth plague (11:1), but the report of its execution is delayed by the insertion of Passover texts (12:1-27). This retardation of the action serves to create suspense for the reader and provides an interpretive key for understanding the tenth plague. The insertion of ritual elements places this plague outside the normal temporal flow of the story; as a result the tenth plague becomes both liturgy and event. Not unlike what a Christmas pageant does to the story, the liturgy/event elides past and present. The Lord brought them *and us* out of Egypt; the saving power of God experienced by the Israelites is made available to each Passover participant. Because the account reflects the details of liturgical practice, it ought not be interpreted as a literal depiction of events. The underlying force of the account is that no household remained untouched by some sort of pestilence epidemic (see the words used for the plague in 9:15; 11:1; 12:13, 23). God works in and through this natural effect of Pharaonic oppression to bring judgment. The Israelites are enabled to leave Egypt "dressed out" in Egyptian valuables, a sign of their new status as free persons, no longer slaves.

The Israelite journey out of Egypt, though carefully planned by God (13:17-22), is interrupted by an Egyptian change of mind (14:5). The Egyptian pursuit endangers Israelite freedom and necessitates further divine action. Liberation from Egypt can truly be confessed only when the threat from the Pharaoh has been fully eliminated. At the same time, God's stated purpose moves beyond Israel's liberation (14:4, 17-18); it has centrally to do with God's relationship to the *Egyptians,* that is, to bring them to the point of knowing that God is the Lord of all the earth. The issue is finally the public honoring of God (9:16). This honor is

Israel's God is cosmic Lord

first bestowed by the Egyptians (14:25), which ironically gives Israel the theme for its public praise (15:1-21). The language of praise entails both language *to* God (adoration) and language *about* God (witness). Without praise, God's victory would not become known before the world, and 15:14-16 begins to show these effects. Indeed, given the cosmic dimensions of the victory, the effects will permeate the natural order in the wilderness (see below).

But the Israelites know more about Pharaoh's plans than God's and proceed to voice complaints (14:11-12). This is the first report of Israel's murmurings, so often voiced in the wanderings yet to come. In response, Moses announces an oracle of salvation: God is at work on their behalf, so they need not be afraid but should stand firm and be silent. God proceeds to work through both Moses (14:16, 21, 26-27) and elements of the nonhuman order (darkness, clouds, wind, waves) to bring about Israel's salvation. At the same time, these elements serve as the vehicle for judgment on the Egyptians, who experience the rebounding effects of their anticreational, genocidal activity. This scene is presented through a kaleidoscope of images that are related to one another impressionistically: divine messengers, pillars of fire and cloud, alternating light and darkness, a strong east wind, the sea cleft in two, walls of water standing up and lying down, a dry sea canyon pathway, bogged-down Egyptian chariots, a lonely human hand twice stretched out, and a shore strewn with dead bodies. It is enough to make a movie mogul's mouth water.

The historical basis for the detail of the account cannot be determined, not least because the surrounding ritual material (13; 15; cf. Joshua 3–4) casts the whole into a liturgical frame of reference and prevents any simple literal reading. This may explain the use of Red Sea language, conveying the cosmic impact of God's work in a way that the (probably actual) crossing of one of the smaller bodies of water in the delta could not. Tidal movements in this region might be a factor, so that one could speak of an unusual confluence of natural and historical possibilities of which God takes advantage. At the least, one can speak of an escape of Israelite slaves from Egyptian control.

The Israelites respond to this liberating work of God in several ways: they revere Yahweh, believe in Yahweh *and* in his servant Moses, and sing two songs of praise to God that celebrate both the historical and the cosmic victory of God. While Miriam's song (15:21) functions as an antiphon in its present setting, it may have been the original song and reflected associated liturgical activity. The people celebrate that God has brought the broken creation back into alignment at one historical spot. A new creation is beginning to take on flesh and blood, and God's reign is once again established (15:18).

The heady days of liberation from Egypt lead immediately into the wilderness (15:22–18:27). A seemingly godforsaken place, the wilderness is far from the promised land of milk and honey. Bondage with security and resources—Egypt—begins to seem preferable to freedom and living from one oasis to another. Trust in God turns to recalcitrance, resentment, and challenges to the leadership of Moses. Yet, even in the face of such realities, God stays with this complaining people and is responsive to their needs. Gifts of food and water (15:22–17:7), deliverance from marauders (17:8-16), and good counsel from nonchosen people deeply affected by God's activity (18) occur in an environment that holds little promise. In the wake of God's cosmic victory at the sea, even the wilderness begins to be transformed to become more of the creation God intended it to be.

Arrival at Mt. Sinai (19:1) issues in a lengthy stay; over eleven months and fifty-eight chapters later Israel departs (Num 10:11). While encamped at the mountain, God takes several key initiatives through the mediating leadership of Moses. God prepares the people for the divine appearance (19), teaches them by means of the Ten Commandments (20:1-17) and the Book of the Covenant (21–23), enters into covenant with them (24), and gives them instructions for building a dwelling place for God (25–31). The introductory section (19:4-6) is central to the entire narrative (see below). Key to what follows in Exodus is the interweaving of law and story (see chapter 5 on Leviticus). Much of the treatment of law occurs in the chapters on Leviticus and Deuteronomy, but a few comments on the Decalogue and the Book of the Covenant are in order here.

The Ten Commandments occur here as the direct address of God and in a slightly different form in Deut 5:6-21; they introduce the two major bodies of law in the Pentateuch, that given at Mt. Sinai (including Exodus 21–23, 34 and Leviticus) and that given on the plains of Moab (Deuteronomy 5–26). As such, the Decalogue

106

provides in apodictic form the "core values" in terms of which the rest of the laws are to be interpreted. These values are concerned most fundamentally with promoting and protecting the life and well-being of the *community*, indeed the good order of creation. The individualized address from the Lord "your" God lifts up the importance of internal motivation within relationship rather than heteronomous imposition or external coercion (no sanctions are stated). Originally, the commandments were all brief and negative in formulation, and have been expanded and adjusted through the years in view of differing community needs. Examples include a change in motivations (cf. Exod 20:9-11 with Deut 5:13-16) and the removal of "wife" from the list of property (cf. Exod 20:17 and Deut 5:21). These changes provide an innerbiblical warrant for ongoing expansion and adjustment (e.g., the coveting command-ment should include husbands as well as wives).

The collection of laws called the Book of the Covenant (21–23) is diverse in form and content. The form ranges from case law (21:26-27) to apodictic declaration (22:28) to divine exhortation (22:21-27) and promise (23:27-28). The content is concerned with ordering a wide range of daily life: sexual ethics (22:19); care of the disadvantaged (22:21-27); worship calendars (23:14-17); loy-alty to Yahweh (20:23). These specific laws draw out the implica-tions of the Decalogue. Developed over time, they are understood, not as a list of laws in force, but as basic principles for shaping the judicial task and the community's life. The admixture of sacred and "secular" throughout is testimony that life is a seamless web and that Israel's God will not be split off to care simply for the reli-gious realm. This integration links actual judicial practice and the work of God in both creation and redemption. All dimensions of life are included for the sake of the good order of God's creation.

Chapter 24 focuses on Israel's response to God in a covenant-making ritual. Its basic elements include a commitment to God's word (vv. 3, 8), various sacrifices (vv. 4-5), the reading of the word (v. 7), the sprinkling of blood as an atoning act (v. 8), and a meal fellowship in the presence of God (vv. 9-11). This God-initiated covenant stands under the umbrella of the Abrahamic covenant (see below). It provides a *closer specification* of what that rela-tionship entails in view of what Israel has become as a *people*. The Sinai covenant is a matter, not of the people's status, but of their *vocation*. God hereby sets this people apart for a task, namely, being faithful to the Word of God in their daily rounds for the sake of the creation.

In 24:12-18, Moses ascends to God's mountain abode and receives the instructions for a tabernacle, a portable sanctuary, and its associated paraphernalia (25–31). Its purpose is to provide a place for God to dwell among the people during their wilderness journeys (25:8; 29:45-46). It constitutes a change in the way God is present among them—ongoing, rather than occasional; close, not distant; on-the-move, not fixed. Yet, the purpose for the sheer volume of detail presented, much of which is repeated in chaps. 35–40 is not at all clear. Perhaps it relates to the situation of the implied audience and their need for detailed future planning for a return to the land where the temple lies in ruins; this could foster a sense of hope. As it once was with Israel and Moses, so it shall be again. At the least, the detail demonstrates the import of God's coming down from the mountain abode to dwell among the people (40:34-38) and the worship of the community centered at the sanctuary. This sets the stage for Leviticus; it provides the place where sacrifices and offerings are to be presented.

Between the God-given instructions for the tabernacle and its construction stand chaps. 32–34. The Israelites take the future into their own hands and compromise their loyalty to Yahweh by constructing an idol in the form of a golden calf (32:1-6). The rest of this section works out the effects of this apostasy. The remaining text centers on a lively dialogue between God and Moses, whose intercession is key to preserving this community from annihilation, if not from judgment altogether (32:9-14, 35), and to gaining assurance of God's presence in their midst (33:1-17). But, finally, the future of Israel is seen to rest in God, who honors human prayer as a genuine contribution to the shape of the future (32:14; 33:17) and, most remarkably, forgives this people and renews the covenant (34:1-10). Such divine responses are grounded in the nature of Israel's God, who proclaims himself to be gracious, merciful, slow to anger, and abounding in steadfast love (34:6-7). Israel's future is seen to be possible only because God is this kind of God.

Emblematic of this new relationship between God and people, the Israelites build the tabernacle precisely according to the divine command, and God descends to dwell in their midst (40:34-38).

NARRATIVE STRUCTURE

The book of Exodus is not to be interpreted in isolation. Its relationship to Genesis is especially important; Exodus is the second chapter of a drama begun in Genesis. This means that the themes of creation, promise, and universal divine purpose, set in place by the Genesis narrative, constitute lenses through which Exodus is to be read (see chapter 2). God's actions on behalf of the oppressed Israelites in Exodus are for the sake of the world, "to make my name resound through all the earth" (9:16).

The relation of Exodus to what follows is also important. The narrative of Israel's stay at Mt. Sinai, begun at Exod 19:1, extends through Leviticus and is not completed until Num 10:10. This means, for example, that the sacrificial system in Leviticus 1–7 is a part of God's response to Israel's sin narrated in Exodus 32–34. In 34:6-7, God announces a change in the divine relation to Israel's sinfulness; for the first time in the biblical narrative, divine forgiveness comes into view. The sacrificial texts take the form of law, but in reality they constitute a word of good news; God thereby provides a means by which the people's sins can be forgiven. This divine action on Israel's behalf goes in tandem with the deliverance from slavery in Exodus 12–15.

At the same time, Exodus 19–40 constitutes a distinct unit within this Sinai narrative complex, and certain structural elements carry theological freight. This unit lifts up themes that are key for the book as a whole: the movement from Israel's servitude to Pharaoh to its service to Yahweh, and from the enforced construction of buildings for Pharaoh to the willing assemblage of a dwelling place for God. Yet, the new master differs from the old, especially in the kind of sovereignty exercised. In comparing such texts as 3:7-10 with 5:5-18 it becomes apparent that *Pharaoh* is the unmoved mover, not God. It is Pharaoh whose heart is hard; God enters deeply into Israel's suffering and is moved by it.

The amount of material in Exodus associated with worship approximates the amount associated with oppression. The details regarding the tabernacle demonstrate the importance of worship and God's special presence related thereto.[3] The tabernacle and God's promise to dwell among the people constitute assurances (verbal and tangible) that God is among them, a gracious divine condescension to the need of the human for that which is concrete and focused. When this theme is combined with Leviticus 1–9, with its provision for forgiveness, these texts constitute a statement that God is both *with* them and *for* them.

This move from slavery to worship means a change in status for the people; it also entails change for God. Exodus begins with an oppressive situation in connection with which God's presence is hardly noted (1–2); it concludes with a statement about God's tabernacling presence in the midst of a sinful people (40:34-38). For God to be so intensely present with a people is a new divine experience. Implicit in these texts (e.g., 25:8; 29:46) is God's "longing" for such an experience (cf. Ps 132:13-14). This move seems to be for God's sake as much as for Israel's. God desires such a "home" among the people! No more mountain hideaways; no more palace precincts. This will enhance the intimacy of the relationship with the people whom God loves. At the same time, it makes for greater vulnerability; God can be more easily hurt by advantages assumed and presumptions advanced. That God does this in the wake of the golden calf debacle (32:1-6) indicates something of the risk God is willing to take for closeness.

The importance of worship is also evident in the interweaving of narrative and worship materials, especially in chaps. 12–15.[4] The reader moves from Passover and unleavened bread (12:1-27a) to narrative (12:27b-42) back to Passover/firstborn/unleavened bread (12:43–13:16) back to narrative (13:17–14:29) to the songs of Moses and Miriam (15:1-21). Liturgy encloses the key salvific events. This structural placement of the worship texts constitutes a liturgical hermeneutic for interpreting the narratives. For example, one is invited to read the account of the tenth plague (12:30-45) through the lens of the provisions given for celebration of Passover (12:1-28). Indeed, this placement of texts means that the final plague is the first observance of Passover; the event itself *is represented as* liturgy. In these narratives an act of God must thus be conceived in both historical and liturgical terms; God is active in salvific ways in both spheres. Even more, the narratives (and Sinai as well) have been shaped by a long history of liturgical practice. Liturgy has shaped this literature.

The structure of chaps. 1–15, as a whole, reinforces this. These chapters are patterned according to a typical lament/thanksgiving structure, familiar from the Psalms (cf. Pss 32; 34). The distress and lament of Exodus (1–2) is followed by God's response in word and deed (3–14) and concludes with a song of praise (15). Characteristic of this pattern is that God acts with specific reference to the stated need within human experience. In this case, God's salvation responds to oppression of a sociopolitical sort and to its adverse effects upon the cosmic order.

Another key structural matter may be seen in the interweaving of law and narrative, especially in chaps. 19–40 (see the discussion of Leviticus in chapter 5). The law does not stand as an external code, separated from the story line. The reader moves from the story (19:1-25) to law (20:1-17) to story (20:18-21) to law (20:22–23:33) to story (24:1-18). Story also breaks into the tabernacle texts at chaps. 32–34. The law is thus integrated with the larger story of Israel and its experience of God's graciousness (the word Torah refers to both law and narrative); the law is given to a people already redeemed. As such, law parallels liturgy in keeping God's activity front and center (see 20:2), enhancing the point that God's purpose in both law and story is "for our lasting good, so as to keep us alive" (Deut 6:24). Law is thereby integrated with life, and is to be obeyed, not just because God says so, but because it serves life and well-being. Even more, law parallels liturgy in that it becomes another way in which Israel responds to what God has done on its behalf.

The structure of Exodus 1–24 also reveals the deep concern for creational matters, especially in parallels to Genesis 1–9: (1) a creational setting (cf. 1:7 with Gen 1:28); (2) anticreational activity, especially violence; (3) Noah and Moses (see 2:1-10; cf. 33:12-17 with Gen 6:8); (4) the flood and plagues as ecological disasters; (5) death and deliverance through water, with cosmic implications; (6) covenant. Moreover, chaps. 25–40 can be understood in terms of a creation/fall/re-creation structure. The story of the golden calf is the story of Israel's fall, followed by acts of divine graciousness and the renewal of covenant (Gen 8:21-22 has rich parallels in Exod 34:9-10).

NARRATIVE THEMES

Exodus 19:3-6 pulls key themes from Exodus together; they provide a lens through which one might view the entire book. "This speech is likely the most programmatic for Israelite faith that we have in the entire tradition of Moses."[5]

111

God's presence

1. *"I bore you on eagles' wings and brought you to myself."* The highly personal terms with which the unit is introduced are of crucial import: I did; I bore you; I brought you to *myself.* Israel's journey beyond liberation is one of being personally borne by God to the special place of God's presence.

Mt. Sinai has been that special place, but God is about to initiate a change of address, namely, the tabernacle. Rather than a fixed place, God will now reside in (and not just appear at) a portable Sinai, a dwelling place in the midst of an on-the-move people, a "mobile home" for God! Rather than being so distant from the people, emphasized by the number of mountain levels Moses ascends to get to God's eaglelike aerie (24:12-18), God descends to be with the people at close range. As noted, this is a new experience for both people and God. God leaves the mountain of remoteness and ineffable majesty, the typical abode for gods in the ancient Near East, and moves into a residence that belongs to the same type (if not quality) as that of the people themselves. No longer are the people—or their mediator—asked to "come up" to God; God "comes down" to them. No more trips up the mountain for Moses! God here begins a "descent" that John 1:14 claims comes to a climax in the Incarnation.

A particular historical experience may lie in the background of these concerns: Israel's dispersion and exile. Questions such as these may have been current: Would Yahweh dwell among such a sinful people? Does the divine purpose still hold (25:8)? Are the divine promises still valid, given the apostasy (29:45)? If Israel understood the golden calf apostasy (32:1-6) as an idolatry like that which led to the exile, the text testifies to the availability of God's forgiveness for a sinful people in *every* historical circumstance, rooted in the very nature of Israel's God (34:6-7). Moreover, the text witnesses to God's perduring relationship with this people through thick and thin, grounded in God's promises (32:13), including the divine choice to dwell among them wherever they may be scattered (40:34-38); God's presence is not to be circumscribed or localized.

These questions lead to others. If a sanctuary is to be rebuilt on the far side of exile, how can this be done so as to minimize the potential for idolatry? Can Israel's worship be structured so as to prevent another debacle? In view of such questions, these texts are conceived programmatically as a return to the time of Moses.

112

As it was in Moses' day, so it shall be again. This blueprint was never realized historically; yet the theology of tabernacle may well have enabled the temple (or *any* sanctuary) to be conceived in less fixed and static terms.

The perspective of 19:4 is summarized in 29:45-46, "I will dwell among the Israelites, and I will be their God. And they shall know that I am the LORD their God, who brought them out of the land of Egypt that I might dwell among them; I am the LORD their God." The God-people relationship is in place throughout chaps. 1–18, the image of the eagle is parental in its range of associations (see Deut 32:10-12), and God's redemptive action has delivered Israel. Yet, God has still further objectives. God's intention for Israel is not just deliverance from slavery, as important as that is. They are now to be ushered into the divine presence, and Yahweh "will be their God" (cf. 6:7).

At the same time, 19:4-6 insists on more than life in God's presence. Faithfulness is crucial in realizing the God-Israel relationship as fully as possible. The personal language continues. Israel is to give heed to "*my* voice" and to keep "*my* covenant." Israel is to be "*my own* possession" and be "*to me*" a kingdom of priests and a holy nation. Israel's response to God is conceived in terms of personal commitment to God himself (no content is given to obedience at this juncture). The emphasis in what follows (reinforced by the "I" language of 20:2-3) has to do with obedience to the one who gives the law rather than to specific commandments in isolation from relationship. Israel is to keep God as the focus of its loyalty and allegiance. Because the law initially comes as direct divine address, as God's word delivered in person, it keeps the law oriented in terms of personal relationship.

This personal character of the relationship between God and Israel is also important in view of the tendency to conceive of the covenant in terms of a contract or a formal agreement. This text raises the issue of obedience within the context of an already existing relationship; relational categories are the fundamental framework within which the law must be conceived. This is reinforced by the fact that the God-Israel relationship has not been without law up to this point; witness pre-Sinai testimonies to the importance of obedience (e.g., 15:25*b*-26; 16:28; 18:16, 20).

Experience has shown that the law can often become an impersonal matter, manifested especially in a debilitating legalism. Law can become a "law unto itself," dissociated from the personal—and hence living and dynamic—will of the law-giver. The narrative, with its interweaving of law and story, reveals a God who is in a lively, pulsating relationship with the people, and hence the law is not to be conceived in fixed or static terms. The God who personally interacts with the people in ever-changing situations throughout their wanderings is the one who gives the law for the sake of the best possible journey.

2. *"You shall be my treasured possession."* To be called God's treasure is to use the language of precious possession for a close relationship (see the use of comparable language with marital imagery in Isa 62:3). Israel is such a treasure now and will continue to be, "if" the covenant is kept (see below). It has been argued that God's choice of Israel took place at Sinai, but this view is unacceptable. Israel has been identified as "my people" throughout the narrative (especially chaps. 3–10), even "my (firstborn) son" (4:22-23). These people are the covenant community that God "remembers" in 2:24 and 6:4-5, the one established with Abraham *and his descendants* (Gen 17:7). The Sinai covenant does not establish the God-Israel relationship. As with other major covenants (Noah, Abraham, David), this one is made with those who have already been elected and delivered, and have responded in faith and worship. Sinai is a more specific covenant within the Abrahamic covenant (which remains in place throughout the narrative, even after the golden calf apostasy [32:13]). As noted, the focus of the Sinai covenant has to do with vocation.

3. *"If you obey my voice and keep my covenant."* The viewpoint that the Sinai covenant is conditional is based upon texts such as these. The nature of conditionality, however, needs further discussion. What does it mean to "obey my voice and keep my covenant"? The reader has encountered this concern about obeying God's voice even before Sinai. The formulation in 15:26, "if you will listen . . . do . . . give heed . . . keep," provides, not a specific law, but a general guideline by which Israel's relationship with God can be tested (15:25; cf. 16:4; 20:20). Obedience is a way of exhibiting trust in the God who speaks the word (for a similar NT perspective, see 1 John 2:3-4). This text (15:26) does not assume that a body of laws exists for Israel, nor does 19:5. Rather, both texts refer to statutes that God may put forward as time goes

on, those that are given as a body (chaps. 20–23) and those that emerge in specific life situations (as in 15:25-26; 16:28; 18:16, 20). Hence, when laws are given at Sinai, Israel knows that they do not exhaust what it means to do the will of God. Sinai fits into a God-Israel relationship in which obedience is already an integral component. Hence, to obey the voice of God is understood to entail more than obeying the laws now to be given.

The phrase "keep my covenant" is not new to the story either; it is integral to the unconditional Abrahamic covenant (Gen 17:9-10), as is "obey my voice" (Gen 22:18; 26:5). To keep covenant is to obey God's voice, but with the more specific reference back to Abraham (note: the use of these phrases does not make the Abrahamic covenant conditional). The only references to covenant in Exodus to this point (2:24; 6:4-5) are Abrahamic, and it is best to so understand 19:5. Israel *as a community* is to respond as Abraham did. The phrase thus has the sense of being faithful to the relationship with God in which the people stand; that is a responsibility more extensive than obedience to the laws now to be given at Sinai.

Hence, the people's response in 19:8 ought not be collapsed into the response in 24:3-7; the former does not yet have the laws of chaps. 20–23 in view. The response of 19:8 is a commitment to obey whatever words God may command over the course of Israel's journey; given the personalism of God's language in 19:4-6, the people's commitment is more to God himself than to specific laws. When the particularization of the Sinai law does come into view, the people respond in terms of their prior promise (24:3-7).

What does "if" mean? There are several possibilities. It could specify a means by which to become God's people; but, as noted, their chosen status is in place. The conditionality could be matter-of-fact in nature: tending to the voice of God will have the effect of an ongoing close relationship. Negatively, it is implied that this closeness could be adversely affected (15:26 speaks of negative effects, but not loss of status as God's people). This seems a likely interpretation, but another dimension is close at hand. The condition is that an unfaithful people would not be the kind of people God calls them to be, bearing forth God's purposes in the world. For Israel to be vocationally faithful, it must obey God's voice and be loyal to the relationship in which it stands. Israel is to keep covenant for the sake of the world (34:10).

Moses' intercession in 32:13 claims that, even in the wake of the golden calf apostasy, the Abrahamic covenant still stands; that God agrees with Moses is clear from the repentance of judgment in 32:14, though it is evident already in God's word about beginning over with Moses (v. 10). God's promise to Abraham (or David [2 Samuel 7]) is not conditional; even Deuteronomic theology holds to such a perspective (Deut 4:31; 30:1-10; Judg 2:1; 1 Sam 12:22). God's promises will never be made null and void as far as God is concerned. Though a generation that rejects God might not live to see the fulfillment of the promise, the promise remains and can be relied on (cf. Lev 26:44-45). God's promise to the community is everlasting, though participation in its fulfillment is not guaranteed to every individual within the community. The promise is always there for the believing to cling to, and such persons can be assured that God will ever be at work to fulfill that promise. The only "condition" is faith itself.

4. *"A Priestly Kingdom and a Holy Nation."* This phrase combines seemingly incompatible images; religious language (priestly; holy) qualifies political images. Words such as kingdom and nation (rather than, say, people or congregation) claim that all aspects of Israel's life are pertinent to the fulfillment of God's purposes, not just the religious sphere. The religious words focus on role. "Priestly" has reference to being mediators between God and the nations not unlike a priest functions in a religious community; holy has reference to a people set apart, not simply *from* other peoples, but *for* a specific purpose. Together, then, the phrases refer to Israel's vocation to be God's people among the nations. The phrases look not inward, but outward beyond the self or the community. This is also the interpretation given by 1 Pet 2:9, which also picks up on Exod 9:16 (and, implicitly, 15:1-21) in its concern for proclaiming the works of God.

Besides vocation, these words also connote inclusiveness. The specific association of the pre-Moses God with "fathers" (see 3:6; 6:3-4; 15:2) is relativized in these verses. Unlike other major covenants (Noah, Abraham-Jacob, David), this one is established with an entire community; the response is spoken by "all" of the people (19:8; 24:3). Both men and women are involved (though 19:15 suggests a focus on males). This inclusive perspective is in tune with the prominent and decisive role of women in the opening chapters (1:15-22; 2:1-10; 3:22; 4:24-26). The phrase, "Let my

116

people go," embraces all Israelites, female and male, children (12:26, 37; 13:8, 14) and adults, slave (13:44; 20:10), and free. The recurring acts of faith, obedience, and worship (as well as despair [6:9] and complaint [14:10-12; 16:2, 9; 17:2]) are ascribed to all the people (4:31; 12:27-28, 50; 14:31; 15:1), and Miriam leads the other women of the community in the great thanksgiving for God's liberating act (15:20-21). The instructions for plundering the Egyptians (3:22; 12:35-36) and for the Passover (12:3) include all the members of the community, and it seems likely that even females are incorporated among the firstborn in 13:1-2.

This inclusive perspective is brought to remarkable expression in 19:4-6, where the entire community is included within God's electing and saving deeds, and priestly language is drawn upon to speak of the vocation of every member. Though the leadership of the worshiping community is given exclusively to males (28:1), this does not diminish the affirmation of 19:6. Worship (an inner-Israelite matter) is not fundamentally what Israel is called to be about among the peoples of the world. All the people of God, not just the (male) priests, are given this vocation: to function among the nations as a priest functions in worship, as mediators of God's blessing (cf. Isa 43:21). This is a strike against any form of (male) clericalism that would claim a special status in seeing to this most basic of responsibilities on the part of the people of God. What this might entail in any given generation in terms of roles cannot be programmed in advance.

Because this statement has such a summary, even propositional character, it has a more foundational role (than, say, 28:1) in evaluating other texts and their continuing import for issues of leadership among the people of God. The more modern phrase, "the priesthood of all believers," has its ultimate roots in this text. Exodus 19:6 might be one of those texts that says more than its original traditionalists imagined (though we have no access to an "original meaning," or any meaning independent of readers); that this is a deliberately subversive passage is also conceivable. In any case, it does relativize surrounding texts (it has an effect comparable to what Gal 3:28 has on, say, 1 Cor 14:34-35) and it provides biblical grounding for a wider role for every person in the religious life of the community.

5. *"Because the whole earth is mine"* (author's translation). Once again, the personal language is used, only this time with refer-

God as creator

ence to the entire earth (cf. Ps 50:11). This phrase has been variously interpreted; indeed, no consensus exists regarding its translation.[6] Many understand it to state the basis for God's choice of Israel rather than some other people. But the use of such language in other texts (e.g., 8:22; 9:14, 16, 29) suggests a more comprehensive sense, best captured in this translation: *Because (kî) the whole earth is mine, so you, you shall be to me a kingdom of priests and a holy nation.* This translation links the text with the missional purpose of God, first articulated in Gen 12:3*b*.[7]

The book of Exodus is creationwide in its scope. Pharaoh's genocidal policies constitute a threat to God's creation, precisely at one point where God has begun to actualize the promise of creation (cf. 1:7 with Gen 1:28). God's response to this threat in the plagues and sea crossing reveals the cosmic purpose that lies behind God's redemptive activity. While God's liberating activity centers on the small community that is Israel, the world provides the horizon in view of which everything takes place. The purpose that informs God's activity encompasses the universe: "to make my name resound through all the earth" (9:16). God's redemptive activity on Israel's behalf is not an end in itself; it is in the service of the entire creation, for "all the earth" is God's. The divine calling to be a kingdom of priests and a holy nation is a commission to a task on behalf of God's earth. God's initially exclusive move is for the sake of a maximally inclusive end.

The nonhuman order gets caught up in these events as much as do people. Much of twentieth-century scholarship, with its stress on God's action in history, has neglected this pervasive dimension in Exodus. To a surprising extent, God works in and through that which is nonhuman, from plagues to sea crossing to wilderness wanderings to the volcanic activity on Mt. Sinai. The plagues, as ecological signs of historical disaster, are used by God to pursue the divine purposes. At the sea, God uses various nonhuman creations—wind, waves, earth, watery deep, darkness, clouds—as agents in and through which God works both judgment and salvation. The nonhuman is the savior of the human! Even more, in the use of images that are basically creational, Exodus 15 confesses that God's victory is not simply a local or historical phenomenon; because what happens at the sea is cosmic in character, it has universal effects. The effect is not simply liberation for the Israelites; God's salvific work affects other gods

(12:12; 15:11; 18:11) and peoples (15:14-16), accomplishes the defeat of anticreational forces, and issues in the reign of God (15:18).

Even more, God's work at the sea begins to effect a transformation of the wilderness. The created order was adversely affected (witness the plagues) by Egyptian anticreational policies. But now, on the far side of cosmic victory, the wilderness springs into new life. The water that could not be drunk in the first plague is now made potable (7:24; 15:23, 27; 17:5-6); the heavens that "rained" hail, destroying food sources, now "rain" bread (9:18, 23; 16:4); instead of the locusts that "come up" and "cover" the ground, destroying plant life (10:14-15), the quails "come up" and "cover" the ground, providing food (16:13; cf. Num 11:31). This transformation of the wilderness does not have a once-and-for-all effect, however, and the prophets will pick up on these images for the transformative effects of God's eschatological victory (e.g., Isa 35:6-7; 41:17-18; 43:19-21; 48:21).

The activity of God as Creator is often associated all too narrowly with the beginning of things, or perhaps extended to include the ongoing divine work of blessing manifest, say, in the growth of flocks and fields. Not as often is the work of the Creator associated with matters of culture and society, and hence law and creation are not often linked. But, the bulk of the law (and here we note especially chaps. 21–23) belongs to the sphere of creation. In view of the symbiotic relationship of cosmic order and social order, so central for Israel (and in the ancient Near East generally), the law was understood in vocational terms, as the means by which the divine ordering of the world at the cosmic level might be actualized in the social sphere. God's will would thereby be done on earth as it is in heaven. The Egyptians, particularly as embodied in the Pharaoh, had subverted the justice of God's world order, "creating" injustice, oppression, and social chaos. God's gift of the law was a means by which the cosmic and social orders could be harmoniously integrated, whereby God's cosmic victory might be realized in all spheres of human interaction.

Finally, we take note of the tabernacle texts and the degree to which they are integrated into this creationwide scope of the book. Verbal and thematic ties between tabernacle and creation have long been noted. Jon Levenson speaks of "the depiction of the sanctuary as a world, that is, an ordered, supportive, and obedient environment," correspondent to the depiction of the cre-ation in Genesis 1.[8] The tabernacle is a microcosm of creation, the world order as God intended it writ small in Israel, a begin-ning in God's mission to bring creation to the point where it is perfectly reflective of the divine will. The worship of God at the tabernacle is a world-creating activity, a God-given way for the community of faith to participate in God's re-creation of a new world, for Israel and for all. Parallels also exist between the tabernacle and the ark of Noah, both of which are viewed as means by which the people of God can move in a secure and ordered way beyond apostasy and through a world of disorder on their way to a new creation (cf. 40:2 with Gen 8:13). And this com-munity on its way can be assured of the continual glory of the divine presence, which is not finally to be confined to Israel, but is to stream out from there into the larger world.

CHAPTER 5

THE BOOK OF LEVITICUS

NATURE AND ORIGIN

The book of Leviticus is the center of the Pentateuch. Inasmuch as worship-related matters dominate the book, this placement may express a conviction regarding the centrality of worship for the life and well-being of the community. As God had been active in Israel's history, so God promised to be active in and through these rituals. In and through these visible and tangible means, from sacrifices to dramatized festivals, God overcame slavery and death for Israel and bestowed life and salvation. Two different dimensions of God's saving action were made available to Israel. Whereas the exodus provided deliverance from the sins of others (this is actualized in the festivals [see Lev 23:42-43]), in the sacrifices, a provision is made for the forgiveness of one's own sin.[1] These gifts enabled a new orientation for life; God's touch in worship gave a new texture to ordinariness. Leviticus has more of a life-giving word and world to offer than its formal character and esoteric content might suggest.

Leviticus may be outlined as follows: offerings and sacrifices (1–7); the priesthood (8–10); issues of purity (11–15); the day of Atonement-Yom Kippur (16); various ritual and moral matters (17–25); a concluding exhortation (26); appendix (27). Chapters 1–16 focus on matters in which the priests are more directly involved; chaps. 17–25 center on behaviors and rituals that promote communal stability in the interrelated spheres of daily life and worship. No sharp division should be made between these two sections, however, as their concerns often overlap (e.g., clean/unclean animals in 11 and 20:25-26; holiness in 11:44-45 and 19).

From early times Leviticus has been considered a Priest's Manual. Yet, while some texts are words of God to the priests (6:8–7:21; 16:1-28; 21:1–22:16), most are directed to "the people of Israel" (e.g., 1:2; 11:2; 17:2); indeed, the concluding summaries are comparably inclusive (26:46; 27:34). Even the materials addressed to priests are laid out for everyone to hear and read in detail. No secret priestly lore exists that is not shared with all; in a kind of democratization, the community as a whole is given ownership and responsibility with respect to these matters.

Critical study of the Pentateuch has shown that Leviticus is part of the Priestly (P) tradition, extending from Genesis 1 to the death of Moses in Deuteronomy 34 (and perhaps beyond). Distinctions within this tradition are often made (e.g., chaps. 17–26, called the Holiness Code [= H], are more hortatory and lay-oriented), but the whole consists of essentially compatible materials.

It has commonly been concluded that these texts are the end-product of centuries of development, having been brought to completion during the exile or after. Yet, several recent efforts have been made to date this material, at least in some form, in an earlier period.[2] One factor contributing to an earlier dating is the existence of complex sacrificial systems in other ancient Near Eastern cultures; Israel's own rituals may have been informed by these cultures from an early time. Generally, these texts may reflect understandings and practices built up over the time of the Solomonic temple (ca. 950–587 BCE). But the present texts seem to have been given a decisive shape during the exile (see 26:34-45) with subsequent redactions likely.

These texts are built back into the Mosaic period, not as a fabrication, but to claim significant continuities with that period in

Israel's worship and life and to provide a paradigm for each generation. For the implied audience, the word may well be: As it once was with Moses and Israel in the wilderness, so shall it be again upon return to the land of promise.

Law and Sinai

Leviticus is a part of that segment of the Pentateuch situated at Sinai (Exod 19:1–Num 10:10). The various statutes are an addition to those of Exodus 21–23 (34); they are given in the wake of the golden calf apostasy and the divine decision to make forgiveness available to the sinful community (Exod 34:6-10). The book of Exodus ends with the sanctuary and associated paraphernalia in place; with the indwelling of God in 40:34-38, it stands ready for use. Leviticus centers on the use of this sanctuary, its becoming operational on behalf of a sinful community, integrated with other statutes regarding Israel's life in worship and world.

The formula, "the Lord spoke to Moses" (or similar) occurs fifty-six times in Leviticus. This introductory word subsumes the various statutes under the will of God, even though Near Eastern sources and priestly reflection have contributed to their formulation. Though Leviticus does not give explicit credit to these human sources and reflections, the Torah tradition does witness to the combination of human insight and divine command (Exod 18:23; Deut 4:6-8; cf. Acts 15:28). Hence, our knowledge of human participation in the development of law does not stand over against the testimony of Leviticus; theologically, one would link such developments to the work of God the Creator both within and without Israel. This divine activity is thus finally the decisive factor, if not the only factor, in the development of Torah.

More specifically, the ordination of priests from the family of Aaron in Leviticus 8–9 precisely follows the instructions given in Exodus 29. The fundamental task of the priesthood in Exodus, to bring Israel to continual remembrance before the Lord (see 28:12, 29–30), stresses their intercessory role, representing the people before God. This role is continued in Leviticus, but in view of the apostasy, their ministry focuses on the mediation of the word and deed of God to the people, especially forgiveness, "making atonement on your behalf" (see 4:20–6:7; 8:34; 17:11; 19:22; cf. 10:10-11).[3]

The Sinai setting continues in the book of Numbers, with

extensive preparations for departure (1:1–10:10), followed by a problematic journey toward the promised land (11–36).

Law and Narrative

The Priestly tradition consists basically of two interwoven types of literature—narrative and law—and thereby it intensifies what is characteristic of the Pentateuch as a whole. The word *Torah* (instruction) refers to both genres. Leviticus contains less narrative in the usual sense, but enough (8–10; 24:10-23) to maintain this feature, particularly when seen as part of the larger Sinai narrative. Narrative features may also be observed in other texts, e.g., the formula at the beginning of most chapters, "The Lord spoke to Moses (Aaron)." This observation is important so that Leviticus is not interpreted narrowly as a law code (and hence more easily dismissed by many) or as static statutes unrelated to Israel's ongoing life. The following interpretive implications for Leviticus (and for the Pentateuch as a whole) are highlighted by this integration of genres:[4]

— law is more clearly seen as another gift of God's graciousness for the sake of life and well-being rather than burden;
— obedience to the law is seen, not as a response to the law as law, but as a response to the story of all that God has done;
— the story shows that the law is given to those already redeemed, as a way of doing justice to the relationship with God in which Israel already stands, not as a means to achieve salvation;
— the law is more personally and relationally conceived when part of a story;
— the law is not to be rigidly fixed, but moves with the story—new occasions teach new duties;
— the story gives to the law a vocational character, a promoting and enhancing of the purposes of God for the creation decisively reclaimed by God's narrative deeds;
— the shape that the law takes in Israel's life is to be measured by the shape of the narrative action of God (be merciful, as God has been merciful);
— the basic motivation for obeying the law is drawn from Israel's narrative experience with God rather than from abstract ethical argument or divine imperative; and

— that God is subject in both law and narrative provides for a continuity of divine purpose, grounded in the personal will of God.

Generally, attention to these implications will mean that Leviticus is not interpreted in static terms, but as part of a dynamic reality within a living community that, at the end of the book, stands ready to move on. Even more, such understandings prepare the reader for Numbers and Deuteronomy, which will introduce new laws for new times and places. While Leviticus will provide a compass for the community during its journeys, it does not promote a myth of certainty, claiming that it knows absolutely what God's will is for every aspect of life. God will have new words to speak in view of life's ongoing twists and turns, for the purpose of the law is the life, health, and well-being of an ever-changing community and each individual therein (see Deut 5:33).

Another genre consideration is the hortatory nature of the material, particularly in chaps. 17–26 (as in Deuteronomy). While this is clearest in chap. 26 (see below), it is evident elsewhere (18:2-5, 24-30; 20:22-26; 22:31-33; 25:18-24). Obviously, this type of material is not compatible with a typical law code, but it correlates well with the interweaving of law and narrative. Such a rhetorical strategy goes beyond a concern to "lay down the law" or "obey because God said so," but intends to persuade, to inculcate, to instill, and to impress upon both mind and heart.

LAW AND CREATION

Israel's law, as with ancient Near Eastern law generally, is most fundamentally associated with creation. This may be observed in the symbiotic relationship between social orders (e.g., family, tribe, nation) and cosmic order.[5] Negatively, disobedience of law has adverse effects in both natural and sociopolitical realms (e.g., Lev 26:19-22, 31-34); positively, obedience is a means by which the divine ordering in creation can be actualized in these same spheres (26:4-10). God's creational order has been disrupted by disobedience and its effects, but God has redeemed Israel and provided means by which Israel can join God in seeking to keep right what God has put right, and to extend that rightness into every sphere of life.

125

To that end, Israel at Sinai is, in effect, addressed as humans were on the sixth day of creation. This may be signaled by the fact that Leviticus begins with a new year (the tabernacle was completed on New Year's Day [Exod 40:2, 17]).[6] In the law, Israel is given tasks in the tradition of the command of Gen 1:26-28: to have dominion over the earth. The law given at Sinai is not a new reality but a fuller particularization of this creational responsibility in view of new times and places, especially given the disruptive effects of sin. Law is a God-given means by which the creation can be made whole once again, integrating the cosmic and social orders harmoniously.

This viewpoint is reinforced by verbal and thematic links between Leviticus and Genesis 1, for example: God's distinguishing and separating in creation (Gen 1:4-7) and priestly responsibility (Lev 10:10); creation "of every kind" in Gen 1:20-25 (cf. Lev 11:14-22); the concern for "seasons" and Sabbath (Gen 1:14; 2:1-3; cf. Lev 23:2-3; 26:2); concern for the land (25:2-5); and a fondness for the number seven (e.g., seven speeches of chaps. 1–7). Israel's tending to such detail links up with God's ordering work in creation and thus takes on universal significance.

This divine objective for making the creation whole again includes laws pertaining to both worship and the broader life of society. Israel's words and deeds in both worship and daily life are world-preserving and world-restoring activities. They are means by which the community of faith can (1) take on the characteristics of that new creation in every aspect of life and (2) participate in the divine work that reaches out to reclaim the creation disrupted by sin and its effects (see below on sacrifice). A recent study by Frank Gorman demonstrates the creational import of these various rituals. Through them, "human beings are called to become participants in the continual renewal and maintenance of the created order."[7] Such activity may be local, but its concerns and effects are cosmic.

In a basic sense, the intentions of God in creation are here understood to be restated, though on the far side of apostasy, and still surrounded by the wilderness. At this small ordered spot in the midst of a disordered world, in and through the various rituals in particular, God begins to work toward the objective of a world that once again can be called "very good." The priests of the sanctuary going about their appointed courses is like everything in creation performing its liturgical service—the sun, the trees, human beings. The people of Israel assuming their creation-given responsibilities in daily life are participants with God in making the whole creation correspondent to the divine intentions.

THE SACRIFICIAL SYSTEM

Leviticus 1–7 (and other texts) speaks of some fifteen different types of offerings. The various details interest few Jewish or Christian readers today. This is understandable, since neither religious group practices what Leviticus preaches. Yet, the theology of sacrifice continues to be significant, not least in the understanding of atonement or the Lord's Supper. The lack of explicit theological statements about its significance, however, complicates any attempt to draw this out; the emphasis in Leviticus is upon implementation. While no thorough review is possible, the following comments set out some basic understandings.

1. The details of historical development are not known, but generally one can say that early on there existed less complexity and greater freedom regarding procedures, places where offerings could be brought, and cultic personnel who could assist (see Exod 20:24). In time, with worship concentrated in Jerusalem, sacrifices became more regulated and priestly-oriented, and uniformity of practice emerged, though perhaps not until the postexilic period. While our present texts probably represent the situation at this latest stage, they reflect centuries of practice.

2. With all the concern about order in these rituals, a certain flexibility is also present. For example, in Lev 5:7-13 the wealth of the offerer is considered in determining the type of offering to be brought. Such openness to difference among worshipers is evidence for a dynamic rather than a static understanding of law. Individual circumstances are taken into account and affect how the law is to be applied and implemented.

3. Not all offerings were animal sacrifices; there were offerings of grain, wine, olive oil, and so forth. Nor were all offerings considered to have expiatory significance; they included offerings of thanksgiving, freewill offerings, and offerings of one's stated "dues" (e.g., tithes, firstfruits). These were expressions of gratitude to God, acts of devotion to God, or acknowledgments of not

only dependence upon God, but of God's claim to all that one has (not unlike modern offerings). They were not "gifts" to God, however, for God cannot be given what is already God's (see Ps 50:9-11). Nor were they considered a feeding of God, though the polemics of Ps 50:12-13 suggests that some so thought (as in some ancient Near Eastern rituals). Basically, these gifts are returned to the Creator in recognition of the experience of divine giftedness, witnessing that the relationship with God was in good order. Certain offerings (especially the sacrifice of well-being) focus on communion, both with God and with others in the community of faith.

4. All but the most heinous sins or disruptions could be forgiven or cleansed or remedied. Even deliberate sins could be atoned for: "you shall be forgiven for any of the things that one may do and incur guilt thereby" (Lev 6:7; cf. 16:16, 21; Num 5:5-10). In such cases, however, the offerings had to be accompanied by full restitution (6:4-5) and explicit confession (Num 5:7; cf. Matt 5:23-24). In the case of "high-handed" sins (see Num 15:30-31), that is, defiant actions by the unrepentant, no such offerings would suffice. Various types of sacrifice related to different offenses.

5. While the instructions regarding such sacrifices are law in a formal sense, in substance they are a gracious offer of forgiveness from God. The people hear in these texts God's promise again and again: Your sins will be forgiven! Hence, this material is well suited to being part of a larger story of freedom from slavery. This is probably the reason that facts considered "inside information" for priestly types are spoken to the people as a whole (Lev 1:2; 4:1). It may be compared to the command to baptize in the Christian tradition.

6. Offerings were not magically conceived, as if they inevitably effected divine favor toward the worshiper. Their efficacy was not inherent in the performance of the ritual. These factors must be taken into account:

(a) God provides the rituals in the first place. God, not human beings, institutes them, thereby graciously providing a tangible means in and through which salvific action might be taken on behalf of the worshiper.

(b) God *in freedom* grants forgiveness to the believer in and through the sacrifice. God freely chooses to recognize sacrifice as a means of grace. The one who brings the offering does not trigger God into action by virtue of what is done in the ritual. God stands ready with forgiveness, but God is not bound to respond favorably to the ritual activity in and of itself.

of course not, but this is not to g____

(c) Contrition and confession of sin are indispensable to the efficacy of the offerings (Lev 5:5-6; Num 5:7; 1 Sam 7:6). H. H. Rowley puts it well: forgiveness "could not be wrested from God by one whose heart was far from him; but it could be claimed by one who approached him in the right spirit."[8] The divine forgiveness is available to one who has faith. The ineffectiveness of the offerings for defiant, unrepentant ones signals the import of the faith of the worshiper. The faith of the worshiper does not "activate" God's response, however. God is freely at work therein.

(d) The importance of the Word of God in connection with the ritual should be noted. This is shown by the presence of a variety of acceptance formulae (Lev 22:23, 25), though we are given no specific texts that were read on such occasions. As G. von Rad states: "Only the addition of the divine word made the material observance what it was meant to be, a real saving event between Yahweh and his people. Only in virtue of the declaratory word did the sacral event become a gracious act of God."[9] Generally speaking, as with the Passover and other festivals, the sacrificial acts were accompanied by the recital of liturgical texts (e.g., 2 Chr 29:27-29; Deut 26:5-11).

(e) These considerations make clear that the commonly drawn distinction between sacrifice and sacrament is not appropriate in connection with Israelite offerings. These sacrifices are actually sacramentally conceived. The gracious role of God throughout makes the phrase, "means of grace," appropriate for understanding what happens in the sacrifices. These are tangible means in and through which God acts in a saving way on behalf of the faithful worshiper. Finally, we are stuck with the word "sacrifice" because it is a literal description of aspects of the ritual.

7. The expiatory dimension of the sacrifices needs further attention. The object of the verb, *expiate* or *make atonement (kipper)*, is sin; it is never God. Whatever the precise sense of the verb, its effect is forgiveness. The language of propitiation (the appeasement of an angry God) is not appropriate.

Leviticus 17:11 is an important verse in moving toward an understanding of this expiatory dimension: "For the life of the flesh is in the blood; and I have given it to you for making atonement for your lives on the altar; for, as life, it is the blood that makes atonement." It is not the blood as blood that is expiatory, but the fact that it bears life. Especially striking here is the statement that the life in the blood has been given *by God.* God himself provides the key element in the sacrifice, namely, the life. Again, the God-centeredness of the rite becomes apparent. Human beings do not bring what is essential for the sacrifice; they are the bearers of a gift from God. Yet, as noted below, what the offerers bring is not inconsequential.

While it was apparently preferred, it was not necessary for life to be taken or blood spilled for expiation to take place (see Lev 5:11-12; cf. Num 31:50; Exod 30:15-16), nor is any special attention or interpretation given to the act of killing. Hence, by definition, expiation did not involve penalty or punishment. The focus was on the rite as a saving event. Moreover, substitutionary language is not explicitly used in these texts; the animal was not considered a substitute for the one who brought the offering.

The ritual of the Day of Atonement is focused both on the cleansing of the people as a whole and of the tabernacle (16:19). Presupposed in this ritual is that sin is not simply to be understood in individual terms; it is a reality that also has a corporate dimension. Thus, the ritual provided a means by which the community as a whole could deal with sin's potential communal destructiveness. To this end, a goat (which was not killed) was sent into the wilderness bearing the sins of all the people (so the term *scapegoat*). This was not understood in substitutionary terms, however; the goat was a symbolic vehicle for dispatching Israel's sins into the depths of the wilderness.

The connections made in Leviticus 5 between the offering brought and what one could afford to bring are also important. The close connection between substance ("wealth") and person suggests that the more wealth one has (in the most comprehensive sense), the more "self" there is to give (2 Sam 24:24, "I will not offer burnt offerings to the LORD my God that cost me nothing"). Thus, in the offering the worshipers submit *themselves* to God in faithfulness. The sacrifice is thus a *tangible sign of faith,* a highly concrete way in which one offers one's self to God; it does not involve some complex understanding of how the worshiper is related to the animal or other type of offering.

Thus it should come as no surprise that, elsewhere in the Old Testament, sacrifices were not considered absolutely necessary for forgiveness (cf. a comparable understanding of the Lord's Supper). Repentance and trust in God were sufficient. This is sharply stated in Ps 51:17, where a "broken and contrite heart" is the crucial human element. This is illustrated in 2 Sam 12:13, where Nathan pronounces absolution upon David following repentance of his sin with Uriah and Bathsheba, with no accompanying sacrifice. Sacrifice and prayer are thus not to stand in opposition to one another. Sacrifice is a form of prayer in which the tangible element is especially prominent and in connection with which God's gift of life and forgiveness has been promised.

From this discussion it would seem that no single theory captures the essence of the sacrificial ritual, whether it be gift or expiation or communion or thanksgiving. If anything, sacrifices center on the saving action of God, which restores the individual and community to life and health in relationship to God and to one another.

Contemporary appropriation of these materials would relate to the theological convictions that inform practice more than the practices themselves. This would include a theology of sacrifice, the understanding of atonement, and the use of visible means in and through which God acts on behalf of the faithful worshiper. Yet, some practices do need continuing attention, for example, the confession of sin and restitution to those wronged.

PURITY LAWS

The priestly material in chaps. 11–15 (and elsewhere, especially in chaps. 17–21) makes two basic distinctions (10:10): holy (that which is brought into a special relationship with God) and common (ordinary, profane); clean (normal) and unclean (anomalous, out of place).[10] These distinctions—and all cultures have them—have to do with appropriate boundaries. The spheres of concern are wide-ranging: animals, and what goes into the body—e.g., blood from the carrion-eaters and carnivores (11); bodily purity, and what comes forth from the body, extended to include clothing and houses—kinds of boundaries (12–15); sacral purity, including times, places, persons, acts, and objects associated with the tabernacle (21), especially idolatry; and moral purity, including bloodshed and sexual relations (17–18; 20).

For Israel, these distinctions have been integrated into the religious sphere. They identify those matters that are pleasing or displeasing to God because they affect the wholeness and stability, indeed the holiness, of the community—with implications for the entire created order—positively or negatively. The priests had the responsibility of making these distinctions (10:10; see Ezek 22:26); they were not so much the boundary setters as the ones who discerned the boundaries set by God, taught them to the people, and presided over rituals of cleansing.

These boundaries of holy/common and clean/unclean are not rigid; they can be crossed, though some entities are permanently holy (God) or unclean (e.g., certain animals; some unclean things can be common). That which is common and clean (the normal condition of most persons and things) can be sanctified and thereby become holy; that which is holy can be profaned and become common; that which is clean can be defiled/polluted and become unclean, but can be purified (some impurities were more serious, e.g., adultery). Temporary forms of uncleanness (from, say, contact with corpses) require cleansing and the passage of time, especially if one is to participate in worship (various rituals are prescribed). The unclean and the holy (both "contagious" to some degree, and one could never be both) are not to come in contact; if they do, certain penalties are exacted and/or forms of cleansing prescribed. Purification and sanctification are divine acts mediated by priests through various rituals by means of which boundaries could be restored and order reestablished in worship and life, indeed for the entire cosmos.

It is important not to translate these distinctions into, say, secular/sacred or dirty/clean or moral/immoral or sinfulness/righteousness. While all sins yielded uncleanness, not all impurities were sins. For example, some impurities are associated with that which is natural and necessary (e.g., sex, death), while others are associated with sin and evil (e.g., idolatry, homicide, illicit sexual relations).

These laws have occasioned various interpretations over the centuries, not least because the text itself provides no explicit rationale. A common suggestion is that the laws serve to separate Israel from the practices of other peoples, a matter of special import to the implied audience (see 18:3, 24). Other factors suggested as rationale for the laws include concerns over personal hygiene, primitive taboos, issues of life and death (note the association of blood and life [17:11]; respect for blood is respect for life, as with semen), and a correlation of social order with cosmic order. An anthropological approach has become common (initiated especially by the work of Mary Douglas).[11] This approach emphasizes social order and wholeness as the key factors that shape the community in life-giving ways. Several of these factors undoubtedly lie behind these purity concerns; they may have been evident to the original practitioners, but certainly these reasons often had been forgotten and participation was informed only by long-standing tradition. The one commonality among the laws now is that they are gathered under the rubric of God's will for Israel. At the same time, the overall purpose of this divine will also informs them, namely, "so that you may live, and that it may go well with you, and that you may live long in the land that you are to possess" (Deut 5:33). Hence, these statutes are put forth because they have the best interests of the community at heart.

Given this fundamental rationale, Christians would seek to appropriate Leviticus in such a way that its concerns would be restated in terms that connect with every new situation in the life of God's people. These concerns would include such wide-ranging matters as food and clothing, housing and disease, sexual relationships, and the character of worship and religious leadership. The issue to be raised: What best serves the relationship with God and the life, health, stability, and flourishing of the community? The consideration of this question would not commonly yield once-and-for-all responses, so the hard work of interpretation and appropriation must be undertaken anew in every generation. A "mixed bag" of examples of appropriation would be the Centers for Disease Control, Habitat for Humanity, laws of sanitation, guidelines for the manipulation of blood, the Food and Drug Administration, seminary worship classes, and ordination candidacy committees.

LAW AND HOLINESS

Leviticus presupposes the holiness language of Exodus, where it is used for everything associated with the tabernacle, including the priests (e.g., Exod 29:44). Especially to be noted is its use in Exod 19:6 (cf. 22:31; 31:13); the people are designated a "holy nation," set apart from other peoples for both a special relationship to God and a role in the world (see chapter 4 on Exodus). At the same time, in preparation for God's special presence, these holy ones must be consecrated (19:10, 14), as were priests (19:22), through rituals of purification.

This understanding remains in place in Leviticus, even on the far side of apostasy; the people are recognized as holy by God (20:26; cf. 22:31-33; 26:12; as were priests by the people [21:8]) and they were to treat themselves as holy (11:44; 20:7) just as God was to be (22:32; cf. Num 20:12). By virtue of this relationship to a holy God and this calling, and by God's sanctifying action (20:8; 21:8; 22:9), the word "holy" becomes a key reference for *all* the people of God (11:44-45; 19:2; 20:7, 26; cf. Num 16:3; Deut 14:2; 26:19), not simply the priests. Yet, the latter seem to have a special holy status ("most holy" [Exod 30:29]) by virtue of their role with respect to the sanctuary and its service (Lev 21:6-8). This closeness to the tabernacling presence of God entailed an intensification of holiness (so also were places and things "most holy" [Exod 26:33-34; Lev 21:22]).

The God of Leviticus is the Holy One who dwells in the midst of this people (Exod 40:34-38; cf. Isa 12:6; Hos 11:9). The holiness of the people (as well as places and things) is directly linked to divine holiness (11:44-45; 19:2); yet, they are genuinely holy. Hence, holiness must be defined basically in terms other than unapproachability or "*wholly* other"; it is a relational category wherein one is drawn into relationship with the holy God, with its benefits and responsibilities, without becoming divine. Strict measures associated with holiness exist not to protect God from contamination by the world, nor to protect the world from God (though violation could mean an experience of divine wrath [10:1-2]), but to honor God's Godness and to assure humans a proper relationship with God in the midst of a world of disorder and sin, a serious matter that God will not take lightly. Once again, exclusive moves are made for the sake of maximally inclusive ends.

It is important to stress that Israel's holiness is a *reality;* it is not something to be aimed at or striven for, or to be associated only with worship. The call to "be holy" is a call to be true to the relationship in which the people already stand (be who you are). The fundamental way in which the people do justice to this relationship is in obeying the commandments, which for Leviticus means being faithful to God in worship *and in life* (see 19:2 and what follows). Israel's holiness is not simply an internal disposition; holistically, it is to be expressed in external ways in every sphere of life. What this entailed may be summed up in Lev 19:18, "You shall love your neighbor as yourself" (19:34 includes the non-Israelite).

The prominent Exodus theme of servanthood also appears in Leviticus and informs the meaning of holiness. The Israelites, God says, are to be "my servants," no longer "their slaves . . . ; I have broken the bars of your yoke and made you walk erect" (25:42, 55; 26:13). The importance of obedience to the divine commands (8:36; 16:34) does not stand over against this divinely given freedom.

In sum, the meaning of holiness is focused on distinctiveness and being set apart through relationship with the indwelling God, as well as serving within a mission that is God's but is set deeply within the world for the purpose of its sanctification.

LAW, COVENANT, AND THE ANCESTRAL PROMISES

Leviticus 26 is a key chapter for understanding what has preceded. Some of its content has been anticipated in earlier hortatory sections (18:2-5, 24-30; 20:22-26). As will be the case in Deuteronomy 28, two possible futures are presented. Initially, the positive possibility is stated (vv. 3-12), and in very personal and relational terms. The purpose of walking in "*my* statutes and . . . *my* commandments" (all that has preceded) is articulated: "I will walk among you, and will be your God, and you shall be my people" (26:12). God will not simply "dwell" among the people, God will "walk" among them (see Gen 3:8; 5:22-24; 6:9). This mutuality in walking suggests a closeness, even intimacy of relationship. This could be read by the implied audience as promissory in character (especially in view of the covenantal language of vv. 42-45). Even the potential judgment is articulated in terms of walking in conflict (26:21-28, 40-41 RSV).

The negative future outlined at greater length (vv. 14-45) is such that the implied audience could see it as descriptive of their recent experience. This future is not as sure as it will be in Deuteronomy 28–32, but it would be *just as clear* for an audience that could read some of the actual details of their own experience on the page. They would understand that the negative possibilities in this chapter have become a reality for them. To the extent that chap. 26 functions as a typical future—that is, possible for any generation—implied readers would be impressed that the negative *has* happened, and hence the potential for it happening *again* needs to be guarded against. The language is almost more matter-of-fact than threat, though it seeks to instill in readers the seriousness of the covenant relationship. The readers' response in worship and life—attending to the center provided by Leviticus— will affect every dimension of their individual and communal lives, positively or negatively.

That the ancestral promises remain in view throughout Leviticus can be seen in the references to the land of promise as the context for life with God (14:34; 18:3; 20:22-24; 23:10; 25:2, 38); chap. 26 picks up on many descendants (26:9), and the covenant with the ancestors (26:9, 15, 42-45; cf. 2:13), including language such as "I will be your God, and you shall be my people" (see 26:12, 45). These references make clear that the covenant is not finally conceived in conditional terms (cf. Exod 32:13; Deut 4:31; 31:1-10). While the people of Israel can break the covenant from their side (26:15), God will not break the covenant with them (26:42, 44). Israel is assured that, even in the face of nonrepentance and consequent experiences of judgment, God will not abandon God's people (26:44-45). This is a word of assurance to an implied audience that lives with deep and enduring questions about the future that might be in store for them.

CHAPTER 6

THE BOOK OF NUMBERS

NATURE AND ORIGIN

Numbers centers on the problems and possibilities of shaping a community identity in tune with God's intentions for the creation. As a long-oppressed community, Israel had a deeply ingrained identity as "slave." Typically, it did not have the resources to move quickly to a "slaves no more" mentality; God was at work enabling them to "walk erect" once again (Lev 26:13). The period of wandering is, at least in part, a necessary buffer between liberation and land for the sake of shaping such an identity. Such an identity does not come easy for Israel or for God; even the most meticulous preparations for the journey are not able to make things go right. One can take the people out of Egypt, but it proves to be more difficult to take Egypt out of the people. The familiar orderliness of Egypt seems preferable to the insecurities of life lived from one oasis to the next. In other words, the problem proves to be not so much the law as an inability to rest back in the arms of the God who has brought freedom and who keeps promises.

The book of Numbers, named for its census lists, is the most complex of the books of the Pentateuch. Various types of literature are represented, for example, lists, itineraries, various statutes, ritual and priestly prescriptions, poetic oracles, wilderness stories, and even a well-known benediction (6:22-27). The interweaving of law and narrative is most evident here, with specific statutes again and again emerging from life situations (see pp. 124-25).

Moreover, some of these texts border on the bizarre, with talking donkeys, curses from a non-Israelite diviner turned into blessings that have messianic implications, the earth swallowing up people, bronze snakes that have healing powers, an almond-producing rod, an execution for picking up sticks on the sabbath, Miriam turning leprous, repulsive instructions for discerning a wife's faithfulness, and a judgment on Moses for very obscure reasons. One is tempted to claim that these strange goings-on were constructed to match the unbelievable character of the community's response to its salvation. To complicate these matters, God is often depicted in ways that challenge traditional understandings; at times it seems as if God's identity is also in the process of being shaped, or reshaped.

The origin of Numbers is also complex. Most scholars consider it to be a composite of sources (oral and written) from various historical periods. The book itself speaks of several sources, including the Book of the Wars of the Lord (21:14) and popular songs (21:17-18; 21:27-30). The tradition most clearly identified and most pervasive is the Priestly writing (in perhaps several redactions), with its interest in matters of worship and priesthood, providing continuity with Exodus 25–40 and Leviticus. Other sources, at times identified with J and E, are more difficult to distinguish, so it is common to speak simply of an older epic tradition. Association of blocks of texts with three primary locales (Sinai, Kadesh, Moab) could reflect a way in which some material was gathered over time. Beyond this, editorial activity seems unusually common.[1]

Also of scholarly import has been the study of individual traditions and their development, for example, the Balaam cycle, the murmuring stories, the censuses, the wilderness encampment, the

Transjordan conquest, the cities of refuge, land apportionment, and the development of the priesthood. It is clear from such work that various Israelite interests from different times and places have in time been brought together to form a unified composition, but the character of that unity has been difficult to discern.

STRUCTURE

The structure of Numbers, often thought to be nonexistent, is best seen from two angles.[2] One focuses on the censuses of chaps. 1 and 26; a second relates to the geography of a journey. These are not mutually exclusive.

The Census Lists

The overarching structure of the book is best seen in terms of the two census lists. The first is that of the generation that experienced the exodus from Egypt and the giving of the law at Sinai. They are now prepared to move toward the land of promise; every command of God has been followed to the letter. When faced with the dangers of entering the land, however, the adults do not trust the promise; they experience God's judgment (14:32-33; 32:6-13), and finally, in the wake of apostasy (a kind of golden calf revisited), die in a plague (25:9). Even Moses and Aaron mistrust God and are prohibited from entering the land; only the faithful scouts, Caleb and Joshua, and the young (14:29) are allowed to do so (26:63-65). The oracles of Balaam (22–24) provide a hopeful sign of things to come, as God blesses the insiders in and through an outsider. These oracles ironically gather the clearest references to the ancestral promises in Numbers (see below); it is almost as if no Israelite, including Moses, has sufficient standing left to bring such a blessing.

The second census (26), with more genealogical detail, lists the members of the new generation (though no birth is reported in Numbers). This generation, as a sign of God's continuing faithfulness to ancestral promises, will enter the promised land. The following texts (27–36) lift up issues comparable to those taken up after the first census, but are now focused on the future in the land. No deaths, no murmurings, no rebellions against the leadership are in view, and various hopeful signs are presented. This new generation is the audience for the book of Deuteronomy.

Journey and Geography

The movement through Numbers can also be tracked in terms of a journey toward the fulfillment of the land promise, with all the problems encountered along the way in spite of careful preparations. Numbers speaks of this journey in terms of key stages, from Sinai through the wilderness—with a long stay at Kadesh—to the plains of Moab east of the Jordan River. Laws are integrated into each segment of the story; they provide for an ongoing ordering of the community as it encounters new situations on its journey toward the divinely promised objective. The positive opening and closing sections enclose a sharply negative picture.

1. *1:1–10:10.* These texts, still set at Sinai, describe various matters that prepare Israel for moving through the wilderness to the land of promise; they bring to a close the Sinai story begun at Exod 19:1. They include a military census (battles are expected), the organization of the camp, and various statutes, especially regarding the sanctuary and its leadership. A somewhat idealistic picture emerges: a community ordered in all ways appropriate to God's dwelling in the center of the camp (5:3); the human implementation of the divine command precisely observed throughout (e.g., 1:17-19, 54; 2:33-34; 3:16, 42). The Aaronic blessing (6:22-27) is given by God to be spoken over the people during a wilderness journey to be led by God himself (9:15-23). One is given to wonder how anything could go wrong.

2. *10:11–25:18.* In episodic fashion, these texts describe stages in Israel's journey through the wilderness; the oasis of Kadesh provides the center of operations for chaps. 13–20. The disjunction between this section and the opening (and closing) chapters is remarkable: obedience to God's command turns to rebellion; trust becomes mistrust; the holy is profaned; order becomes disorder; the future of the people of God is threatened. Integrated with these journey reports are miscellaneous statutes, focused on purification, the need for which grows out of these experiences (15; 18; 19). They are "perpetual statutes throughout your generations" (e.g., 15:15; 18:8; 19:21), so they constitute a hopeful sign, as do the oracles of Balaam. As with the first section, the texts do not function simply as stories of the past; they speak to future generations of the people of God—including the implied audience.

3. *26:1–36:13.* This entirely positive segment reflects a time of waiting for the land. As in the prior sections, statutes are woven into the story, especially regarding worship, vows, land apportionment and boundaries, levitical cities, cities of refuge, and inheritance issues. These concerns anticipate the future time in the land of promise, where God will (continue to) dwell among the people (35:34); the community is to so order its life that this dwelling place of both God and people shall not be defiled and polluted (a word with renewed import in the modern world!).

KEY THEMES

Certain themes provide compass points for negotiating the journey through Numbers; we present them as questions in view of the many questions in the book. These themes will enable the reader to look, in a somewhat circular fashion, at Numbers texts from varying perspectives.

Why Have You Brought Us Up Out of Egypt? (20:5)

The book of Numbers presupposes that God is committed to the ancestral promises. Generally, God has "promised good to Israel" (10:29). More particularly, the promise of land is emphasized.[3] As Israel moves out from Sinai, the goal is the land that God is "giving" (10:29; 14:16; 32:11 and often). Conditions regarding fulfillment of the land promise are expressed (14:8), but they affect the future of individuals—even an entire generation—but not finally Israel as such (14:22-24, 30-31; 20:12). Beyond that, the promises are spoken almost exclusively by Balaam: a great nation with kings (24:7-9, 17-19); blessing (22:12; 23:20; 24:9); to be God to them (15:41; 23:21-23), and many descendants (23:10). It is ironic that Balaam, the outsider, rather than rebellious Israel, expresses these promises most clearly; indeed, he forcefully speaks of God as a promise keeper (23:19).

The book's middle section (11–25) complicates the movement toward fulfillment. The scouts, sent to spy out the land of Canaan (13–14), bring back a mixed report. It is a bountiful land, but ten scouts (of twelve) bring back "an unfavorable report of the land" (13:32), despising God's own gift; they also voice alarm at the strength of its inhabitants. Rather than rejoice in the minority report of Caleb and Joshua of "an exceedingly good land" (14:7) and trust that God will see to the promise (14:9), the people are seduced by the negative report (14:36) and plead to return to Egypt (14:1-4); they even call *Egypt* the "land flowing with milk and honey" (16:13)! Again and again, they look back rather than forward; they trust the deceptive securities of the past more than God's promised future (11:5; 21:5). Hence, they experience disasters that threaten progress toward the goal, including plagues (11:33), an abortive conquest (13–14), and snake infestation (21:6). Balaam seems to be one of the few who trusts where the exodus from Egypt is heading (23:22-24; 24:8, 17-19).

On the other hand, chaps. 26–36, with the new generation in place, bespeak confidence in the promises with the apportionment of lands not yet conquered (26:53-56; 33:51-56) and the specification of the land's boundaries (34:1-15). Even anticipated inheritance problems are covered (27:1-11; 36:1-12). These and other laws (15; 18; 19), while put in place to handle emerging issues, constitute a hopeful sign in the midst of much failure and grief; they imply that a community will exist to attend to such matters. This is especially evident in 15:2; in spite of Israel's infidelities, land possession is assumed and laws are given for that time. In some sense, the ongoing promulgation of law is a witness that the promise of land will indeed be fulfilled.

Numbers had begun with preparations for battle (1:3); the land would not be Israel's without a fight (unlike the sea crossing in Exodus). Successful battles take place around the edges of Canaan proper, for both generations (21:1-3, 21-32; 31:1–32:42). These initial conquests and the settlements in the Transjordan function as a "down payment" on the complete fulfillment of the promise. These successes provide an element of hope regarding the future; this is the beginning of what shall be. At the same time, the possibility of future loss of the land is hinted at (33:56; 35:33-34), a theme struck already in Leviticus 26 and again in Deuteronomy 28–32.

Did I Conceive All This People? (11:12)

God, not Moses, has birthed this "family" and has chosen to stay with them; indeed, to dwell in the very heart of their camp. From this womblike center, blessings flow out into the encircled community. This intense presence is promised for the land as well (35:34). Even the non-Israelite Balaam testifies to the presence of such a God among the people (23:21-22) and the Egyptians have heard of it (14:14).

Israel's God not only dwells among them but also goes before them. As in Exodus (13:21-22), the accompanying presence of God is associated with the pillar of cloud/fire; in fact, 9:15-23 speaks of this symbol of God's presence in such a way that the itinerary is not predictable or routinized. This symbol is linked to the ark of the covenant, which represents the presence of God (10:35-36). If the ark did not accompany the people in battle, then defeat was inevitable (14:39-45), though the ark is not necessarily associated with victory (21:1-3; 31:1-12). While only one text mentions human guidance in the wilderness (Hobab [10:29-32]), its placement before the ark text (10:33-36) suggests that both human and divine factors are important for the journey that now follows (Hobab's descendants will settle in Canaan [Judg 1:16]).

Because of the intense presence of God, the tabernacle was protected from casual contact. The tribe of Levi was consecrated for service at the tabernacle, was camped around it (1:50-53), and was responsible for guarding this holy place. Any person who intruded into these sacred precincts was to be executed (1:51; 3:10, 38; 16:13; 18:7); indeed, even Levites could die if the furnishings were mishandled (4:17-20; cf. Lev 10:1-3).

Looming large over these developments are past infidelities, especially the golden calf debacle, where Israel violated its relationship with God and jeopardized its future (Exod 32.9-10). In the wake of this near disaster, God still graciously chose to dwell among the people; but, given the people's propensity to apostasy, safeguards had to be instituted so that a recurrence might be prevented. Israel has been honored by this incredible divine condescension for the sake of intimacy in relationship, but God remains God and this divine move is not to be presumed upon. It may be said that this very closeness of God and people would make for an even deeper trauma should something go wrong with the relationship (see Amos 3:2).

Israel's time in the wilderness is finally shaped by God's extraordinary patience and mercy, and the divine will to stay with Israel in this time of their adolescence as children of God. Coping with adolescents is no easy task, even if the parent is God (cf. Hos 6:4). No divine flick of the wrist is capable of straightening them out without compromising their freedom. If God wants a mature child, the possibility of defiance must be risked. Parent and child even do a certain amount of "testing" of each other (see Deut 8:2). But it soon becomes clear that the process of maturation will take longer than a single generation. God will not compromise in holding Israel to high standards.

In view of the creational interests we have been tracking in the Pentateuch, these standards are put forth for the sake of the future of the creation. God's broader concern for the reclamation of the entire creation is evident in the provision of food and water in the wilderness (11; 20), as in Exodus 15–17.[4] But Israel's despising of God's gifts (11:5-6, 18) and the lack of trust Moses and Aaron exemplify relative to the accessibility of such gifts (20:10-12) subvert God's creational intentions. Balaam's blessing of Israel and his knowledge regarding God's promises (see above) show that God is able to work in and through outsiders to further the divine purposes; indeed, given the rebelliousness of the chosen, God may be compelled to take that route.

The birthing imagery for God (11:11-14) is another creational motif Numbers brings to the Pentateuch. God is "The God of the spirits of all flesh" (16:22; 27:16), not just of Israel. Indeed, Israel's election and God's promises are for the sake of the creation (see 14:21, "the earth shall be filled with the glory of the LORD"; cf. Isa 11:9). This may inform Moses' concern about God's reputation among the Egyptians, indeed "the nations" (14:13-17).

Has the Lord Spoken Only Through Moses? (12:2)

Divine revelation is not confined to the people's stay at Sinai or to the book of Deuteronomy; it takes place throughout Israel's journey. God's word is usually mediated through Moses, but not uniquely so. Indeed, the issue of who speaks for God becomes an issue during the journey. This issue is an ever contemporary one, so readers ought not be surprised at this, and implied readers no doubt could see their own situation reflected here. Challenges to Moses' leadership by the people had begun already in the pre-Sinai wanderings (Exod 16:8; 17:2); they are intensified in Numbers, when other leaders also take up the argument.

The issue is voiced most sharply by Miriam and Aaron: Has God spoken only through Moses? Has he not spoken through us also? ([12:2] a related challenge is pursued in 16:3, see below). The answer to the first question had been given in 11:16-30. God's

144

spirit resting on Moses was shared with seventy elders (even with the two who had stayed in camp, Eldad and Medad); they proceed to prophesy, if only once. Moses abruptly puts down those who would try to stop such speaking: "would that all the LORD's people were prophets!" (v. 29). When God speaks to Miriam and Aaron (12:5-8; cf. Mic 6:4), God acknowledges such communications. God's spirit will rest upon Joshua (27:18) and it even rests upon the outsider Balaam who mediates the Word of God (24:2-4, 15-16). God is not captive to a one-way street into this community; indeed, if need be, God will go around the chosen ones to get a word through. But Moses does have a special relationship with God, so that challenges to his role are not countenanced, and Miriam suffers for it (but not Aaron!), as does the entire first generation of Israelites.

God communicates to and through Moses often in Numbers (e.g., 15; 17–19); indeed, 7:89 speaks of Moses' contact with God in an almost routinized way. In 12:8 God himself claims for Moses a unique mouth-to-mouth or face-to-face encounter (see Exod 33:11; Deut 34:10). Moses actually "beholds the form of Yahweh" (as in Exod 24:9-11) and lives to tell about it. Exodus 33:7-11 spoke of the tent of meeting at which God appeared in a cloud to speak to Moses. The tabernacle functions in this way also in Numbers (11:25; 12:5; 14:10; 16:19, 42; 20:6; cf. Deut 31:15). The word *glory (kabod)* speaks of the fiery radiance within the cloud (cloud and glory are combined in 16:42; Exod 16:10). References to the angel of God (Exod 14:19; 23:20; cf. 3:2) suggest a human form within the flame of fire that God assumes for the sake of personal encounter.

One facet of God's relationship with Moses needs special attention: the genuine interaction between them as they engage issues confronting the wandering community. This was characteristic of their relationship in Exodus (3–6; 32–34), and Moses' intercessory activity intensifies in Numbers (11:2; 12:13; 21:7). Indeed, Moses (in the tradition of Abraham before Sodom and Gomorrah) challenges God with questions (11:10-15, 21-22; 14:13-20; 16:22; cf. Ps 106:23). This discloses something about both God (see below) and Moses. Moses' capacity for leadership is considerable, including a capacity to tolerate threats to his authority (11:29; 12:1-2). Moses calls forth the narrator's strong statement on his unique humility (12:3; cf. Deut 34:7-12). Aaron and his sons also

145

take actions that have an intercessory function; in 16:48 they stand "between the dead and the living" and a plague is averted (cf. 25:7-13). This correlates with their mediating role in rituals of purification (5; 15). Interest in the proper succession of leaders (Eleazar [20:22-29]; Joshua [27:12-23]) also demonstrates the crucial importance of leaders for the stability of the community.

Several theological considerations regarding the divine revelation may be useful at this point:

1. God's word has a visible, even tangible aspect. For the people (who actually *see* the cloud/glory [14:10; 16:19; cf. Lev 9:6, 23]), it serves to authenticate the *external* origin of the word (even if they do not hear it). The word comes from God, not from Moses' own mind. This is a way of guarding against possible misuse of religious authority, a too easy use of the claim "God spoke to me." No cloud/glory, no word from God.

2. This means of revelation discloses a basic way in which God relates to the world. God clothes himself in created reality and appears to speak. The finite is capable of the infinite. This is done so that God can be present as concretely and personally and intensely as possible. But this less than overwhelming way also means for God a more vulnerable presence, for the human response can be derision or incredulity or mistrust (e.g., 20:12).

3. Moses remains key to God's word being mediated *and interpreted* to the community. God's concern for clarity in hearing and seeing is stressed in 12:6-8. Individuals enjoy a communicative capacity that cannot be shared equally by an entire community. Even more, differences exist among leaders; Moses has a mediatorial status not enjoyed by (other) prophetic figures (see Deut 34:10).

4. Commandments and statutes enjoin Israel all along its journey. This was the case with Israel's wanderings *before* Sinai as well (15:26; 18:23). God's word is not delivered in a once-and-for-all fashion at one time and place; God's revealing is a dynamic reality, intersecting with life and all of its contingencies (see chapter 7 on Deuteronomy).

5. God's relationship with Moses is one of integrity. God invites Moses into conversation and is open to what he has to say; God honors Moses' contribution as an important ingredient for shaping the future of the issue at stake. Indeed, God may move from (preliminary) decisions made in view of such interaction (14:19-

20). But such divine openness to the future will always be in the service of God's unchanging goals for Israel and the creation.[5]

Why Then Do You Exalt Yourselves Above the Assembly? (16:3)

The prominent call in Leviticus for the people to be holy (= to be in life who they are in fact) is continued here (15:40). What constitutes a holy life, or that which is inimical to it, is essentially continuous with that set out in Leviticus. Hence, various uncleannesses—whether moral or ritual—are incompatible with holiness, from bodily discharges and contact with a corpse (see 5:2; 31:19) to illicit sexual relations (5:19). For such violations, various purification rituals are provided (see 15; 19; 31:19-24; 5:1-10).

A sign of Israel's status as a holy people is a blue cord on the fringe of each person's garment ([15:37-41] still worn on prayer shawls by orthodox men). The dispute that follows is instructive. Korah's claim (16:3) that "every one" in the camp (and the Lord) is holy is not incorrect; the problem is the implication he draws, namely, that Aaron (and also Moses) has no special prerogatives for ministry in the sanctuary. Moses' reply assumes gradations of holiness; even if all are holy, God chooses from among them those who are to exercise priestly leadership, and this chosen status constitutes a holiness that sets them apart from other holy ones (the Nazirites are another class of [temporarily] set-apart holy ones [6:8]). The disaster experienced by Korah and his company (16:23-35) proves the special status of both Moses (16:28-29) and Aaron (16:40).

Gradations of holiness are also evident within the members of the tribe of Levi. As noted, the Levites are set aside to care for the tabernacle; this is symbolized by their encampment between the tabernacle and the rest of the people. Laws relating to them are unique to Numbers (e.g., 3–4; 8:5-26). They represent Israel before God, and indeed they are substitutes for the firstborn of all Israelites (3:11-13); the effect of this is that the demarcation between "lay" and "clerical" is somewhat blurred. Among the Levites the family of Aaron was especially set aside for priestly duties (16:40; 18:7-11, 19), about which Leviticus was concerned. The legend of Aaron's blossoming staff (17) conveys this point of view in the wake of the challenge of chap. 16. Moreover, a special "covenant of perpetual priesthood" is made with this family because of the mediatorial actions of Phinehas, Aaron's grandson and Eleazar's son (25:10-13). The distinctive status of this family can be seen in its role in the succession of Joshua to the Mosaic office, and in its God-given role of mediating the Word of God; even Joshua "shall stand before Eleazar the priest" (27:21).[6]

Rebellion against God-chosen leaders is seen to be deeply subversive of God's intentions for the community and risks death short of the goal. Even Moses and Aaron are not exempt from strict standards; indeed, the reasons given for their being prohibited from entering the land seem almost trivial (20:10-12). It may be that such leaders are held to a higher standard of conduct than others, not least because the impact of their mistakes has such a deep and pervasive effect on the community.

How Long Shall This Wicked Congregation Complain Against Me? (14:27)

Finally, we return to focus on the theme of wilderness. The texts associated with Sinai come to a close at Num 10:10. The opening chapters have ordered the community in all essential respects. A unified people moves away from Sinai, with each tribe having equal status and bearing equal responsibility within the community (1:3; 13:2). The remaining chapters observe how they respond when they encounter the wilderness. The picture that emerges is not attractive. The well-ordered community quickly succumbs to discord and disarray; it begins to mirror the wilderness through which it is wandering. The summary in Numbers 33 reviews forty stages in the wanderings, but the actual route is uncertain; only a few can be identified with any confidence.

But even the Sinai stay is considered a wilderness experience (Exod 19:1; Num 10:12); the law is given in the wilderness, not in Egypt or Jerusalem, and the various statutes that emerge during the wanderings shape the community in view of ongoing experience. By 22:1 the people are "across the Jordan from Jericho," and there they remain to the end of the Pentateuch; they are still in the wilderness. In its total impression, especially if one keeps the journeying ancestors in view, the Pentateuch is a wilderness book. The word wilderness says something very basic about the ongoing life of the people of God. As such, it is a book with special import for the implied audience that experiences wilderness in either literal terms or symbolic terms or both.

The wilderness stories in Numbers are similar in form and

content to those in Exodus 15–18; once again we hear of manna, rocks producing water, battles with desert tribes, and seemingly nonstop complaints. Yet, Numbers is different. The complaints in Exodus are tolerated, as if in consideration that a long-oppressed people is entitled to some grumbling. Numbers expresses and assesses the people's complaints differently, perhaps because of the golden calf apostasy. The themes of sin, repentance, and divine judgment, not present in the Exodus wanderings, become prominent in Numbers. The people are sharply identified as rebellious, against both God (and what God has done) and Moses/Aaron. These recurring failures threaten the well-being of the community and its relationship with God; the judgment of God is invited into the picture again and again.

Israel's rebellious murmurings and the resultant divine judgment are confined to the middle section of Numbers (11–25). The very first stage of the journey is depicted in these terms (11:1-3), as is the last (25:1-18), and virtually every stop in between. Insufficient detail is given in these texts to probe very deeply into the dynamics of sin and divine judgment. But chap. 14, a key chapter in the move from old generation to new, may provide an understanding that fits most cases.

The people sharply complain (14:2-4) and persist in their rebellion in spite of pleas and acts of contrition from their leaders (14:5-10). God's response has several dimensions:

1. God voices a lament (14:11), echoing those of people and Moses (11:11-14), using language familiar from the psalms (Ps 13:1-2). The reader is thereby given a glimpse into the divine heart; God does not remain coolly unaffected. The judgment that follows is spoken not with the icy indifference of a judge, but with the mixed sorrow and anger of a lover who has been wounded. That God's lament is repeated in v. 26, interrupting the announcement of judgment, reinforces this understanding.[7]

2. God announces a disastrous judgment, but will start over again with Moses. We know from what follows (cf. Num 16:20-21; Exod 32:9-14) that this is a preliminary judgment, a point for debate, for entering into conversation with Moses (see above). At the same time, such judgment would be fully deserved.

3. God enters into conversation with Moses (vv. 13-35). Moses argues (as in Exod 32:11-14) that God's reputation among the nations is at stake; he quotes God's climactic statement from that

previous interaction (Exod 34:6-7), pleading for God to forgive the people as God had often done. In other texts, human intercession may be reported as prayer (11:2; 21:7) or action that "turned back my wrath from the Israelites" (25:11) or action that diminished the effects of a plague (16:46-50).

4. God responds favorably to Moses and forgives Israel (14:20); but forgiveness, while it ameliorates the effects of sin (they are not annihilated), does not cut off all consequences. Hence, the old generation dies in the wilderness and their children suffer the results of the adults' infidelity (14:33). This reality is true for all acts of forgiveness; the consequences of sin, which can affect the innocent, need ongoing salvific attention (e.g., abusers may be forgiven, but the effects of the abuse do not thereby disappear). Chapter 21:4-9 provides another illustration: Even though the people had repented (and presumably had been forgiven), the snakes are not removed nor kept from biting. In other words, the effects of sin continue, but God works on those effects by providing a means (a homeopathic Egyptian technique with which the promise of God is associated) in and through which to heal those who are bitten (cf. the combination of prayer and medicine in 2 Kgs 20:1-7).

5. God announces the judgment (14:21-25) and, after another lament, details that judgment in moral order terms ("what goes around comes around" [14:28-35]). A key verse is 14:28, "I will do to you the very things I heard you say." In effect: your will be done, not mine. Their desire for death in the wilderness (v. 2) is granted (vv. 32-33); their desire for a return to Egypt ([vv. 3-4] a reversal of the exodus!) is brought close to hand (v. 25); their claim that their children would become booty in the land (v. 3) leads the children to suffer that fate at their parents' own hands (v. 33); they want different leaders (v. 4), they will get them (v. 30). Here judgment is understood to be intrinsic to the evil deed; God does not introduce it into the situation. God is not arbitrary, but facilitates a consequence that correlates with the deed. One might speak of a wearing down of the divine patience in view of 14:22; the other side of the coin is that persistent negative human conduct will in time take its toll, and God will see to the proper functioning of the moral order. If we had this kind of detail in relation to the other sin and judgment stories, it is likely that a comparable understanding would be forthcoming.

Such a portrayal mirrors the situation of the implied exilic audience in a special way. Their rebellion and apostasy and the resultant experience of divine judgment lies in their recent past; talk of old and new generations would be especially pertinent as the years of exile in the wilderness moved by.

The New Testament picks up on two different themes from Numbers: (1) it cites God's providential care for Israel in the wilderness; and (2) it lifts up Israel's infidelity as a warning for the people of God in every age. These themes are carefully interwoven in 1 Cor 10:1-13, where some ten texts from Numbers 11–25 are referenced; it is carefully noted that these passages were "written down to instruct us" (cf. Heb 3:7–4:11; Jude 5-11).

CHAPTER 7

THE BOOK OF
DEUTERONOMY

NATURE AND ORIGIN

Deuteronomy is both an ending and a beginning; it looks both backward and forward (see chapter 2). It recalls the ancestral promises and the exodus deliverance, retells events experienced by the people at Sinai and in the wilderness, and looks forward to the time in the promised land (and even beyond). Deuteronomy is a pivotal book; it provides an interpretive lens through which the reader is invited to interpret what precedes and what follows.

Deuteronomy, which means "second law," comes from the Greek translation of a Hebrew phrase in 17:18, "copy of [the] law." This translation correctly carries the idea that Deuteronomy is a law that follows upon that given at Sinai (29:1). The phrase also recognizes that Deuteronomy repeats and recasts various matters from previous books: stories regarding Sinai and the wilderness wanderings as well as numerous laws from Exodus, including the Decalogue. Moreover, the phrase conveys a key characteristic of the law more generally: God's law is not a matter given once and for all. Law was integral to life before Sinai and develops after Sinai in view of the needs of new times and places. The phrase also suggests that Deuteronomy has an authoritative role in how the first law is to be interpreted; hence its association with Moses. But this is more a theological claim than a historical one, for example, Deuteronomy is in authoritative continuity with the law given by God to Moses at Sinai and is to be given a comparable status in the community (cf. the relationship between the U.S. Constitution and its amendments).

Regarding the origin and formation of Deuteronomy there is both agreement and dispute. Substantial agreement is evident in linking (a form of) Deuteronomy with the lawbook that 2 Kings 22–23 reports was found in the Temple during a reform in the reign of Josiah (640–609 BCE). Profoundly moved by this book in view of the disparity between its contents and Israel's religious practice, Josiah intensified his reform efforts. The close correspondence between these efforts and the content of Deuteronomy supports this link (e.g., the suppression of idolatry and the centralization of worship). Another point of agreement is Deuteronomy's relationship to Joshua, Judges, 1 and 2 Samuel, and 1 and 2 Kings (Dtr). As noted (see chapter 2), the literary style and theological perspective of Deuteronomy is continued in Dtr. The opening section (1:1–4:40) may have been composed to introduce the entire corpus. In addition, Deuteronomic influence is evident in the redaction of some prophetic books, particularly Jeremiah. Scholars also speak of Deuteronomic editing in Genesis–Numbers, though less agreement exists as to its extent.

This widespread evidence, which covers a considerable range of Old Testament material, suggests that something on the order of a Deuteronomic School was at work on Israel's traditions during the eighth-sixth centuries BCE. The identification of these leaders is disputed, however; candidates include prophets, scribes, Levites, and religious officials in Jerusalem. The hortatory style and the interest in Israel's spiritual life point toward those charged with the ongoing responsibilities of preaching and teaching. Catechetical interests are prominent, and a prophetic edge is also evident in the strong call to attend to the needs of the poor and needy. A theological agenda pervades the entire book, but it is an applied theology, concerned to move the hearts and minds of the audience. At heart, the book focuses on the proper relationship between Israel and its God, essential if Israel is to have a future. It is likely that the book should be associated with a circle of like-minded individuals, drawn from several leadership groups, who were steeped in Israel's religious traditions and deeply committed to its spiritual health.

Although scholars agree that Deuteronomy developed over a considerable period of time, less consensus exists regarding details. One plausible scenario: a core of the material is to be tracked back to religious centers in the Northern Kingdom; after the destruction of the north in 721 BCE, dispossessed leaders fled south with their traditions. There they joined with other sympathetic leaders, and together they were instrumental in the abortive reform efforts under Hezekiah (2 Kgs 18:1-8). Forced underground during the reign of the apostate Manasseh (687–642 BCE), they resurfaced under Josiah. But the hopes for reform were dashed with the death of Josiah in 609 BCE and increasing military pressures from the Babylonians, which led to the destruction of Jerusalem in 587 BCE and the exile to Babylon. Yet, these traditions continued to be nurtured over the years, for the destruction and the exile seem to be known to the framers of the book (4:25-31; 28–31; see chapter 2). So, one might speak of a series of expansions to a basic core of the book (perhaps the bulk of chaps. 12–26) that took place over the course of a century and more, being brought to completion in the wake of the catastrophic events of 587 BCE.

These historical developments may explain something of the depth of the warnings of the book and the need for a response that is both spiritual and political; indeed, Israel's very survival seems to be at stake. At the same time, a somewhat idealistic picture of Israel is presented that pushes beyond historical specifics and becomes applicable to *every generation of Israelites.* As 5:3 puts it, "Not with our ancestors did the LORD make this covenant, but *with us,* who are all of us here alive today" (italics mine). Every generation would understand that the "with us" applied to them and that they were the addressees of both the laws and the promises. Each generation was to place its hope in a God who would fulfill promises and make the people dwell secure in the land (30:1-10). On this actualizing tendency, see the discussion in chapter 2.

STRUCTURE

Up to this point the Pentateuch has presented the law as the word of God to Moses (except the Decalogue); here it is presented as the word of Moses to Israel, and hence a more public word. This elevates the status of Moses, but more basically it lifts up the role of the human in the continuing task of interpreting the word of God. Even more, it presents a certain rhetorical strategy for bringing that word of God to *public* expression. Three overlapping structures of the book are commonly delineated.[1]

The Addresses of Moses

One structure is provided by *the addresses of Moses* to the new generation on the last day of his life; the speeches mediate the word of God to a people about to enter the land of promise. Superscriptions set out the addresses, perhaps as many as six (1:1-5; 4:44-49; 6:1; 12:1; 29:1; 33:1).

1. *Chapters 1:1–4:43.* Basically, this segment consists of remembrances of Israel's journey from Sinai to Transjordan; it gives a realistic picture of a people whose loyalty to God is deeply divided. Chapters 29–32 will contain a comparable portrayal. The section concludes with an exhortation on the importance of faithfulness in view of both divine command and divine promise (4:1-40), and an appendix regarding cities of refuge (4:41-43). The entire text is personalized in such a way that every generation can identify with the "you" or the "us/we." Many interpreters think that this segment originally introduced the entire Deuteronomic History (perhaps in two stages, with chap. 4 added later).

2. *Chapters 4:44–5:33.* The initial words (5:3) make clear that the new generation stands in fundamental continuity with the old in terms of the divine commands and commitments. The Decalogue (5:1-21) not only introduces the segment, but, as the only laws spoken (and written!) directly by God to the people, it sets the core values or enduring values for all laws that follow (and, by implication, any other laws that might be developed over time). As such, its redactional placement and function are exactly

the same as the Decalogue in Exodus 20. These two (slightly different) Decalogues introduce and ground the two major law complexes of the Pentateuch mediated by Moses: Exodus 20, the laws given at Sinai; Deuteronomy 5, the laws given on the plains of Moab. In other words, all Pentateuchal law is to be understood through the interpretive lens provided by the values of the Decalogue. The reason for the giving of the law is stated clearly: it is a gracious divine gift "so that you may live, and that it may go well with you, and that you may live long in the land" (5:33).

3. *Chapters 6:1–11:32.* These chapters are hortatory addresses focused on the centrality of the first commandment. They are introduced by the Shema ("Hear" [6:4-5]): "Hear, O Israel: The LORD is our God, the LORD alone. You shall love the LORD your God with all your heart, and with all your soul, and with all your might." This is, in essence, a restatement of the first commandment (5:6-7), centering on the centrality of faithfulness to the one and only God. To love with heart, soul, and might engages the entire person in a decisive, passionate, and intense fidelity to this God and to no other. This commandment will definitively shape the telling of Israel's story that follows (Dtr); this commandment will reveal the root of Israel's history of failure (see chapter 2). At the same time, it provides Jesus with language to speak of the center of the faith (Luke 10:27).

Chapters 6–11 explore what this fidelity entails from various perspectives, including historical retrospects, making very clear where the heart of the matter lies for Israel and for God. Dennis Olson considers the issue of idolatry to be less culture specific than might first be thought, including the "gods" of militarism, materialism, and moralism.[2] The section comes to a climax in a key question, "So now, . . .what does the LORD your God require of you?" (10:12). The powerful response in 10:13-22 pulls together the integral relationship between love of God and love of "stranger" (cf. Lev 19:18, 34; a combination also used by Jesus [Mark 12:28-31]), grounded and motivated in God's saving deeds.

In the following statutes something of what God requires when it comes to love of God and love of neighbor are specified. These statutes do not exhaust the meaning of love, but they do provide direction.

4. *Chapters 12:1–28:68.* This section contains various statutes that more closely specify the core values of the Decalogue for life

in the land of promise. This section reflects a more settled and institutionalized community than does Exodus 21–23. The statutes in chaps. 12–26 are introduced and concluded with matters of worship; the kind of relationship one has with God is key to all other relationships. Chapter 12 stresses the centralization of Israel's worship life as a strategy for protecting Israel's faithfulness; chap. 26 emphasizes that life in the land is to be centered in a grateful response to all that God has done. These chapters bracket a series of laws that encompass the myriad of life's detail, including the character of leadership, various religious and social institutions, the conduct of war, food and clothing, property and animals, and marriage and family life. Woven throughout are special concerns for the first commandment and care for the less fortunate (the widow, the orphan, the resident alien, the Levite). The hortatory rhetoric is especially intense when these persons come into view (read 15:1-11). Life with God and life with the other are inextricably interconnected.

This section concludes with blessings and curses that stress the seriousness of Israel's relationship with God and with the other (27–28). The language of the curses is strong, even repulsive (e.g., cannibalism), but those who know something of the history of the twentieth century—from "ethnic cleansing" to the ravishing of the environment—know that the consequences of human sin can be devastating (see below). What Israelites say and do in the various aspects of their daily life truly counts for something; the future of Israel, indeed, the future of the entire creation is at stake.

5. *Chapters 29–32 and 33–34.* The centerpiece of the final sections is a second covenant, established with the new generation as a supplement to the Sinai Covenant (29–30), followed by various covenant-making provisions (31) and words and acts designed to provide for a future upon the death of Moses (32–34). For further comments about the function of these segments, see chapter 2.

Commandments and Statutes

A second structure relates to *the ordering* of commandments and statutes. As noted, one should speak of only two major complexes of law in the final redaction of the Pentateuch: (a) those given at Sinai—primarily Exodus 21–23 and Leviticus; and (b) those mediated by Moses on the plains of Moab—Deuteronomy. Each of these complexes is now introduced by the Decalogue (Exodus 20; Deuteronomy 5). The Decalogue provides the core or enduring values that undergird and inform the statutes that follow them. These core values are not absolutely immutable, as the change in the coveting commandment from Exod 20:17 to Deut 5:21 demonstrates, but they are relatively more stable (cf. 4:2). In Deuteronomy the arrangement of the statutes in chaps. 12–26 appears to follow the ordering of the Decalogue; they proceed to give "commentary" on each of the commandments in turn, though not explicitly or precisely so.[3]

"Book of the Covenant"

A third level of structure in Deuteronomy is provided by its character as a "book of the covenant" (2 Kgs 23:2). The book itself speaks of two covenants, one at Sinai (5:2) and one in the plains of Moab (29:1). The new generation has already participated in the former (5:3); the Moab covenant, which is not mentioned elsewhere in the Old Testament, supplements the Sinai covenant.

Some elements of a structure comparable to ancient Near Eastern treaties may be observed in chaps. 1–28: historical prologue (1–3), covenant stipulations (12–26), and blessings and curses (27–28). Also to be noted are the provisions for witnesses, periodic reading, the transference from an oral word to a written word, and its deposit in the ark (31). The latter chapter, however, is related to *both* the covenant at Sinai and the one at Moab, which is set forth in chaps. 29–30 and has a different structure.

Though ancient Near Eastern treaty connections are present, they have less substantive import than commonly has been suggested. Generally, it is important to stress that *covenant is a metaphor*, and as such does not fully comprehend the relationship between God and people (every metaphor has a "yes" and a "no"). The covenant between God and Israel is much too personally and relationally construed for treaty or agreement language to do it justice. For example, God is not bound to respond to Israel in strictly legal or contractual terms; God is free to exercise patience and mercy.

The covenant in Moab creates an even greater distance from the Near Eastern treaty; it is essentially a renewal of the *Abrahamic* covenant (29:13; cf. 4:31), and it plays a role here not

unlike its role in Exod 32:13 in the wake of the golden calf debacle. The covenant recognizes that Israel will fail to keep the Sinai
covenant, but that God's "sworn oath" (see 29:12, 14) will not let
that failure rule the future (see Lev 26:40-45). Judgment will in
fact fall, but this covenant assures the people that "when all these
things have happened" (30:1), that is, on the far side of judgment,
exile, *and* repentance, God will "[transform] the curse into blessing, the command into promise, and the stipulation into gift."[4]
For example, the command that the people circumcise their
hearts (10:16) becomes a promise that God will do that; God will
enable the people to be obedient once again and the land will
prosper (30:6-10; cf. 29:4). The move into the future entails settlement in the land, removal from the land, and resettlement in
the land.

Chapter 31 makes provision for a written form of these
covenants for the continuing community and its leadership;
chaps. 32–33 poetically sketch the dynamic between old and new
that is at work. The song of Moses in chap. 32 provides a "witness
against" (see 31:21; 32:46) the people's failure in the face of God's
gracious work in their midst; it is parallel to the law itself (31:26).
Chapter 33 fills out the blessings that will follow upon God's
actions in 30:1-10 and as announced in 32:34-43: "The LORD will
vindicate his people," but only "when he sees that their power is
gone" (that is, beyond judgment). God's people will live within
the tension provided by certain failure and judgment and certain
promise and restoration to the land beyond judgment.

Deuteronomy has cast both covenants in liturgical terms. In
the report about a formal act of promising (26:16-19), both God
and people publicly state certain obligations with respect to the
other. The repeated "this day, today" (cf. 5:3) stresses its intergenerational character. After symbolic provisions for future reference (27:1-8), the divine declaration is made: "this very day you
have become the people of the LORD your God" (27:9). The Moab
covenant (beginning in 29:1) is reported in comparable terms
(29:10-15), except the people make *no response* (though they are
called to observe it [29:9]); it is a unilateral divine oath. A
renewed call to obedience is made so that the commandments
are not relaxed (30:11-20), but the response is left open-ended.
This is liturgical language, perhaps associated with covenant
renewal rituals; it does not mean, for example, that the Israelites

had not been God's people up to this point. Rather, every generation (29:14-15) must claim both promise and obligation anew for themselves and hear anew the declaration that they are God's people. They cannot simply rest on the commitments made by any past generation. The faith cannot be transmitted by genetics (cf. Gen 22:16-18); at the same time, in the face of human failure and beyond judgment, God will see to a future for this people.

PURPOSE

Discerning the purpose of Deuteronomy is difficult, not least because its genre is not self-evident. *Torah* is the most common self-description, but its use shows that it means more than law or statute, or even instruction in its basic sense. In 1:5 and 4:44 Moses is to set forth the *torah,* but what follows is mostly story (1–3) and hortatory address (6–11). Even in chaps. 12–26 the word "law" does not adequately express what is presented (read, e.g., 15:1-11). This book would not have constituted a code to be used for legal decisions by Israelite judges or elders. The statutes are considered more as witnesses to the will of God than prescriptions with statutory force. The hortatory rhetoric, in particular, suggests that existing statutes constituted but one source for a more fundamental agenda.

The purpose of Deuteronomy relates to the needs of the new generation (Numbers 26). These people not only need to be taught the basics of the tradition, they must take this knowledge to heart and live in accordance with it, if they are to move into the future with courage and confidence (Josh 1:7-9). Careful attention to "the words of this *torah*" is crucial, not only in view of the infidelity of the old generation, but also because of their own sinful propensities (Deut 31:21-29).

In view of such an agenda, Deuteronomy might be called a religious education tract or a reform document. Dennis Olson's designation of catechesis is helpful, "a foundational and ongoing teaching document necessitated by the reality of human death and the need to pass the faith on to another generation."[5] Yet, for all the focus on teaching (e.g., 4:5), the heart of the book's concern seems more explicitly religious; the tradition is not simply to be taught but to be inwardly appropriated. It is not simply a matter of the *fides quae* (the content of the faith), but of the *fides qua* (faith itself). The very relationship with God is at stake; nothing could be more fundamental. Deuteronomy 6:2-9 puts it this way, "that you and your children and your children's children may fear the LORD your God all the days of your life, and keep all his decrees and his commandments." Hence, Deuteronomy might be understood as *spiritual direction.* Such a phrase more adequately describes a book that is so personal in its religious expression and so rich in its spiritual depth. This spirituality, however, is not simply inward-looking or God-directed; it incorporates a lively concern for a faith that is active in love, especially toward the less advantaged. Moreover, in the face of all that is potentially destructive of this spirituality, all of Israel's individual and institutional resources (e.g., judges, kings, priests, prophets [16:18–18:22]) must be readied to protect it.

This purpose is cast in intergenerational terms (6:2-9; cf. 4:9-10; 11:19). Not only are the people to keep these words in their own hearts, they are to transmit these words to the next generation; they are to recite them, talk about them in every walk of life, write them down, and display them on their very selves and on their property so that others can see them. Even the questions of children are brought into play (6:20-25; cf. Exod 12:26; 13:14-15; Josh 4:6-7, 21-24): "When your children ask you in time to come, 'What is the meaning of the decrees . . . that the LORD our God has commanded you?' then you shall say to your children, 'We were Pharaoh's slaves in Egypt, but the LORD brought us out of Egypt with a mighty hand . . . to fear the LORD our God.' " The book is not designed simply to transmit a fixed tradition; it is concerned about the *meaning and appropriation* of that tradition down through the ages.

In addition, what Moses has said is to be written down and read every seventh year to the entire community: "Assemble the people—men, women, and children, as well as the aliens residing in your towns—so that (note the interest in the *fides qua*) they may hear and learn to fear the LORD your God and to observe diligently all the words of this law, and so that their children, who have not known it, may hear and learn to fear the LORD your God" (31:12-13; cf. Neh 8:8).

In service of this purpose, Moses employs a certain rhetorical strategy for impressing these materials upon both heart and mind (see chapter 2). This material is presented, at least initially, as orally delivered addresses, not as written documents. The book is directed to "you," to "the heart," "today." The language is relational, and is personalized for everyone. Its use of vocatives and its calls to hear and heed, to watch and remember, are designed to engage the reader at more than intellectual levels. The "you" is at times singular and at times plural, perhaps as a device to engage readers in both their individual and communal levels of self-understanding. These texts are a form of persuasive speech.

KEY THEMES

Deuteronomy is a theologically rich book, as has been evident above and in chapter 2. Several of its other key themes are noted in the following discussion.

The Ancestral Promises

For Deuteronomy, the people of Israel are one people, chosen by God (Deut 7:6-8; 14:2). This language of election, usually used for kings (17:15) and priests (18:5; 21:5), has been extended to refer to the people as a whole. This election is grounded in God's choice of the ancestors *and their descendants* (4:37; 10:15; cf. Gen 17:1-8). The command Moses places before Israel to "choose life" (30:19) presupposes this divine choice and Israel's status as God's people; having been chosen, Israel can now choose. The statutes are given to a people already in relationship with God to shape their callings in every walk of life. They are never understood as a means to establish, preserve, or reestablish the relationship with God.

God makes promises to those whom God chooses. For all of the references to law, Deuteronomy's pages are full of promises. God *swore* these promises to the ancestors (over thirty instances); God put God's own life on the line for the sake of the promises (see Gen 15:17-21; 22:16). The most prominent promise in Deuteronomy is the promise of the land.[6] It is set from the beginning (1:8) and reaffirmed at the end (34:4). Everything put forth in the book depends on the fulfillment of this promise; Israel's future with God always comes back to the land.

The promise of the land extends even beyond judgment. That the land will be possessed in the near future is a certainty (e.g., 26:3, "I have come into the land"). Yet a loss of the land is just as certain; Israel will prove unfaithful and forfeit it (28:63-64; 29:28). At the same time, beyond judgment, God promises that Israel will be restored to the land (30:1-5). So, in effect, the promise of land has a double horizon for Israel in Deuteronomy—a near future and a distant future.

Deuteronomy's land promise assumes the fulfillment of other ancestral promises—many descendants, nationhood, divine presence, blessing, and relationship (1:10-11; 2:7; 4:20; 7:12-13; 10:22; 13:17; 15:4-6; 26:5, 15-19; 28:9-13; 29:10-13; 30:16). Some of these promises have already been fulfilled (many descendants [1:10-11]), and they also extend into the future.[7] The fulfillments will not lapse.

For all the importance of the past in Deuteronomy, what is at stake is the identity and character of the community as it moves into the future. Israel must diligently observe God's statutes in the land they are about to possess (12:1). What people say and do will make a difference, not only to their own future, but to the future of God. The nature of the future divine action (whether blessing or curse) will be, at least in part, contingent upon Israel's response to the will of God for life. Israel's future will depend finally on God's promise, but that does not relieve Israel from the responsibility of a faithful life. What is at stake here is not only the life and health of Israel, but that of the entire creation.

Law, Redemption, and Creation

The statutes God gives Israel are understood basically in creational and vocational terms.[8] That is, the statutes are grounded in God's work in creation and they serve God's creational purposes of life, stability, and the well-being of individuals and communities. To this vocation Israel is called, for the sake of the creation. The law is not created by the exodus; Mosaic law is a fuller particularization of the law that is implicitly or explicitly commanded in creation (Gen 1:28; 2:16-17; 9:1-7) for a newly redeemed people (see chapter 2).

God's redemptive work is a decisive reality undergirding Israel's vocation, but it is important to remember that the divine objective is the reclamation of creation. In attending to the law, Israel joins God in seeking to keep right what God has put right, and to extend that rightness into every sphere of life. To that end, God's redemptive work empowers Israel in its vocation and provides paradigms and motivations for Israel's obedience (see below). The range of Deuteronomy's concern in this regard is remarkable; it moves through social and natural orders and includes relationships with other nations and their gods.

1. *The Social Order.* One basic creational/vocational concern for Israel has to do with the social order. Deuteronomy understands clearly that human life is at odds with what God intended in creation. The law is a means by which the divine ordering at the cosmic level is actualized in the social sphere.

Many of Deuteronomy's concerns can be associated with the stability of the community and its flourishing, for example, provisions made for rituals and worship (14:1–16:17), institutions with appropriate leadership (16:18–21:14), and marriage and family (21:15-21; 22:13-30; 24:1-5; 25:5-10). A special interest is evident in the recurring refrain: the widow, the orphan, and the resident alien (e.g., 24:17-22). This concern for the underprivileged probably reflects the devastation of the Northern Kingdom (721 BCE) and the near demise of the south, when Israel's armies were decimated by the Assyrians. But in the present text this lively concern for the poor and the needy has been generalized: "There will never cease to be some in need on the earth" (15:11). This sets an ongoing vocation for the people of God and God has provided sufficient blessings to overcome this reality (15:4).

The laws that seek to protect and nurture the poor and the needy are considered among the oldest in the Old Testament. While also attested in ancient Near Eastern law, their frequency in the Old Testament and the intensity with which they are presented demonstrates their unparalleled significance for both God and Israel. Caring for the disadvantaged is more a theological matter for Israel than a sociological or a political one; these commands come from God, not from "city hall," and the integrity of God's creation is at stake in the way in which these people are cared for. One could claim that social justice issues, for all their "liberal" associations, are thereby given a deeply "conservative" cast (so also the common appeal of the prophets to these traditions, e.g., Isa 3:13-15).

The passion with which this concern is presented shows how far Deuteronomy moves beyond a law code. This energy has its roots in older law; see Exod 22:21-27: "You shall not wrong or oppress . . . [or] abuse. . . . If you do . . . I [God] will kill you." The intensity can be seen in Deut. 15:1-11, with its strong hortatory language: "Do not be hard-hearted or tight-fisted toward your needy neighbor . . . willingly [lend] enough to meet the need. . . . Give liberally and be ungrudging." The law is not simply to be obeyed; an open and generous attitude must inform obedience. This concern is to be manifested in very specific ways: food (24:19-22; cf. 23:24-25), daily wages (24:14-15), loans and interest (24:10-13; 23:19-20), release from debt repayment (15:1-11), and justice in the courts (24:17-18; 16:18-20). Even more, the needy were to be drawn into the heart of Israel's worship life (16:11-14; 26:11; cf. 5:14). While slavery, inconsistently, remains a part of Israel's life and shows the pressure of economic interests (15:12-18), a humanitarian concern is evident (cf. Exod 21:1-11).

2. *Land and Animals.* Another basic aspect of Deuteronomy's creational/vocational concern has to do with the land. Descriptions of "the land of milk and honey" promised to Israel are numerous (6:10-11; 7:13-14; 8:7-10; 11:10-15; 28:1-14; 30:9; 32:13-14; 33:13-16, 28). This bounty includes the land itself (hills and valleys), iron and copper, water from within the earth and timely rainfall, herds and flocks, and grains, vines, and fruit trees. All this is a gift from the Creator, a sacred trust from God. These resources are not developed by the Israelites themselves, so they cannot boast (8:17-18); they have no "natural right" to use them as they please. The language throughout is in the continuing present tense: the Lord your God *continues* to give the land. Israel's response was to be taken up at various levels: to confess publicly that God is giver (26:1-11), to set apart a tithe of the produce (14:22-29), and to tend and nurture these gifts. Such tending is to range widely, perhaps grounded in the sabbath rest for the animals (5:14; cf. Exod 23:12). The people's responsibilities are to include caring for stray or hurt or hungry animals (22:1-4; 25:4; cf. Lev 25:7), protecting mother birds for the sake of producing further young (22:6-7) as well as fruit-bearing trees when a city is under siege (20:19-20; cf. Lev 19:23-25), and providing rest for the land (see Exod 23:10-11; Lev 25:2-7).

Though these gifts are in fact available apart from Israel's doing, they will not *remain* available if Israel is not faithful to its relationship with God (11:16-17; 28:22-24, 38-42, 51; 29:22-27; 32:22-24). Moral order affects cosmic order. Moreover, unfaithfulness does not simply entail Israel's removal from the land and

165

this abundance, but the *land itself* will suffer. These texts want to make an ecological statement. For example, 11:17 links infidelity to the absence of rain and an unfruitful land; 28:22-23, 38-42 links disobedience to drought, blight, insects, worms, and turning the land into a dust bowl; 29:22-27 links abandonment of the covenant with burned-out soil unable to support vegetation. This linkage has been a theme since Gen 3:18, where thorns and this-tles grow in the wake of human sin (cf. Hos 4:1-3).

The text does not make explicit the nature of the connection between such effects and the anger of God (11:17; 29:23-27; 32:22) or the divine curse (28:15-68), that is, how the divine anger is mediated (28:49-57 does speak of other nations). Yet, the lan-guage of the curse "coming upon, pursuing, overtaking" (see 28:15, 45) suggests an inexorability about sin's consequences. That is, God does not introduce these effects; they grow out of the actions themselves (cf. the plagues in Exodus 7–11, here experi-enced by Israel). Yet, God is not removed from this process (e.g., 28:58-68). God sees to the moral order that God built into the cre-ated order (perhaps this complex reality is conveyed by the fact that some verses speak of God as agent, while others do not). Generally, this vision of disaster is rooted in experience, both that of Israel (Assyrian and Babylonian sieges) and that of other peo-ples (many of the curses have parallels in ancient Near Eastern treaty documents). Those with ecological sensitivities will recog-nize modern parallels here; for example, the link between human behavior and polluted natural resources (with rebounding effects upon human health).

The covenant in Moab, with the blessing of Moses (29–33), moves beyond such disasters and envisions a new day when the land will again be fruitful and yield its increase (30:9; 33:13-16, 19, 28). The land will participate with the people in the effects of God's new day of blessing and salvation (cf. Isa 35:1-10).

3. *Other Nations.* God's creationwide purposes are also evident in the way other nations are drawn into the conversation. The God who created human beings (4:32), who is God of heaven and earth (4:36, 39; 10:14), drives out nations before Israel (4:34, 38; 7:21-22). God rules over the nations in such a way that Israel can be chosen from among them (7:6-8). But this does not mean that God ceases to care for these peoples. God gives lands to the out-siders (Edomites, Moabites, and Ammonites [2:5, 9, 19]), indeed

dispossesses peoples to do so; explicit parallels to Israel are drawn (2:12). God is active in the world independent of Israel, working deeds of care and deliverance (cf. Amos 9:7). In fact, Israel is dependent upon such peoples for their life (2:6) and needs to be alert that God can work through them *against* Israel (1:44; 28:48-49).

The outsiders are also given a role as observers and assessors of God's work. In 4:6-8 the nations look at Israel's observance of the commandments and conclude that they are a "wise and discerning" people (cf. 26:19). Implicitly, the commandments serve as a witness to God among other peoples. In 29:24-28 the questions and the conclusions of the nations regarding divine judgment are given theological stature: These outsiders will know that the judgment has come because Israel has been unfaithful to God. In 32:26-27 (see also 9:28), God is concerned about how such outsiders might respond to acts of divine judgment. In 4:32-34 other peoples are to be asked whether the activity of Israel's God can be compared to any other. This seems to assume the idea, evident in 29:26 and 32:8-9 (cf. 4:19), that Israel's God in creation had allotted other gods to other nations. Such statements retain a remarkable openness to religious expressions other than Israel's; indeed they claim that Israel's God built such a religious pluralism into the created order, while at the same time insisting that for Israel there is no other God besides Yahweh (32:39).

At the same time, Deuteronomy contains texts such as 7:1-2 (cf. 2:34 and 3:6 with 20:13-14) which are virtually genocidal in their ferocity toward others. While such actions are grounded in a concern about infidelity and extreme danger to the future of the community (7:4; 20:18), and unfaithful Israel did not remove itself from the line of fire (28:15-68), they remain incomprehensible to most modern religious sensibilities. Perhaps the above reflections on the nations begin already to subvert such ideas internally.[9]

4. *Paradigms and Motivations.* The motivational language commonly associated with the statutes in Deuteronomy has basically to do with a reclamation of creation: long life, peace and stability, healthy and prosperous individuals and communities, and a thriving natural order. It is not enough to say that the laws come from God, and that alone gives Israel sufficient reason to obey. Rather, God gives Israel reasons to obey the law that are linked to creation.

At one level, obedience is in *Israel's* own best interests. Again and again, Israel is to obey "so that you may live, and that it may go well with you, and that you may live long in the land that you are to possess" (5:33; cf. 4:40). God commanded the law "for our lasting good, so as to keep us alive" (6:24). The concern is not to bind Israel to some arbitrary set of laws, but to enable the people to experience the fullness of life, health, well-being, and the flourishing of their communities. To obey the law is seen as something eminently reasonable; any right-thinking person could hardly do otherwise. Even outsiders recognize this (4:6): "Surely this great nation is a wise and discerning people!" To obey the law, then, is finally to trust that God knows what is best for individual and community.

Sometimes readers interpret this language in terms of rewards, as if obedience would be divinely rewarded with well-being and long life (cf. 5:16). Rather, life and well-being are intrinsically related to obedience; that is, they grow out of the deed (as in the case of negative effects, noted above). To live like this will, as a matter of course, issue in such effects; that is the way God made the world to work. Such effects are not inevitable, of course; life is not that consistent. But, generally speaking, obedience will lead to a fuller life, more in tune with God's creational intentions.

At another level, obedience is in the best interests of *the marginalized and the outsider.* As 10:18-19 puts it: God "loves the strangers, providing them food and clothing. You shall also love the stranger, for you were strangers in the land of Egypt" (cf. 15:15). Israel's obedience is motivated by a personal experience with the God who issues the command, but the objective is the well-being of those who have not yet received the effects of God's reclaiming work. Israelites are to extend mercy to the needy just as God was merciful to them when they were in such straits. This could be called an ethic of gratitude, but basically it has to do with extending the life and well-being that Israel has received to those who have yet to receive them.

This motivation is important because (among other things) it makes clear that obedience of the law for Israel is not a means to right relationship with God. As the introduction to the Decalogue shows (5:6), these statutes are given to those already redeemed. Thus, the law does not introduce a new form of slavery; indeed, it is a means by which Israel mediates God's creation-reclaiming work to those still held in one kind of bondage or another.

The Dynamic Character of Israel's Law

Finally, we note that Israel's law is not a static reality, intended to remain the same for all times and places. For Israel and for God, new occasions teach new duties. The following factors from previous discussion may serve as a conclusion.

The integration of law and narrative throughout the Pentateuch (see chapter 5 on Leviticus) is a key consideration. God's gift of the law is not drawn into a code, but remains integrated with the story of God's gracious activity in the ever-changing history of God's people. Law is always intersecting with life as it is, filled with contingency and change, with complexity and ambiguity. Law takes experience into account while remaining constant in its objective: the best life for as many as possible. This means that new laws will be needed and older laws will need to be recast or set aside. For example, Deuteronomy reflects later Israelite institutions such as prophecy (13:1; 18:15) and kingship (17:18). Moreover, the admixture of civil, moral, and cultic laws within the texts shows that, unlike a modern tendency, life was not separated into such neat categories; the will of God had to do with every sphere of life. So, various types of law from diverse life settings have been integrated into a single fabric, but they relate to one another in ways that are not always clear to moderns (e.g., the sequence in 22:4-6). In the service of life, the law is as complex and as dynamic as the God-people-world interrelationship.

Another important factor is the relationship between laws in Exodus and Deuteronomy. Some nineteen statutes from Exodus 21–23 are recast in Deuteronomy.[10] For instance, the laws concerning slaves in Exod 21:1-11 have been revised in Deut 15:12-18; in 15:17, for example, one is to "do the same with regard to your female slave." Internal tensions and inconsistencies between these laws, however, are not ironed out or considered a threat to the law's integrity. Rather, old and new remain side by side as a canonical witness to the process of unfolding law. Hence, *development in the law* is just as canonical as individual laws or the body of law as whole. At the same time, all remain the laws of God—older words from God and newer words from God. Just because laws are from God does not make them immutable; but the retention of both in the canon means that each such word from God is to be considered carefully in moving toward any new formulation.

Hence, instead of an immutable, timeless law, the text witnesses to a developing process in which experience in every sphere of life is drawn into the orbit of the law (compare the development of motor vehicle or tax laws). This ongoing formulation of new laws is in tune with the divine intention, and some of those laws (like their biblical predecessors) may well stand over against existing biblical statutes; but this should happen only after a thorough and careful consideration of the old.

NOTES

1. THE STUDY OF THE PENTATEUCH

1. For these and similar questions, see J. Blenkinsopp, *The Pentateuch* (New York: Doubleday, 1992). See also R. N. Whybray, *Introduction to the Pentateuch* (Grand Rapids: Eerdmans, 1995).

2. See W. R. Tate, *Biblical Interpretation: An Integrated Approach* (Peabody, MA: Hendrickson, 1991).

3. C. Holladay, "Contemporary Methods of Reading the Bible," in *The New Interpreter's Bible,* vol. 1 (Nashville: Abingdon, 1994), p. 128.

4. For a survey of these and other approaches, see J. Barton, *Reading the Old Testament: Method in Biblical Study* (Philadelphia: Westminster, 1984).

5. Originally published in German in 1878; the second edition of 1883 was translated into English in 1885 and reprinted as *Prolegomena to the History of Ancient Israel* (New York: Meridian, 1957).

6. See R. E. Friedman, "Torah (Pentateuch)," *Anchor Bible Dictionary,* vol. 6 (New York: Doubleday, 1992), 6:605-22.

7. The introduction to Gunkel's 1901 commentary on Genesis has been translated, *The Legends of Genesis* (New York: Schocken, 1964).

8. See G. von Rad, "The Form-Critical Problem of the Hexateuch," in *The Problem of the Hexateuch and Other Essays* (New York: McGraw-Hill; Edinburgh: Oliver & Boyd, 1966), pp. 1-78.

9. M. Noth, *A History of Pentateuchal Traditions* (Englewood Cliffs, NJ: Prentice-Hall, 1972).

10. A. Alt, "The Origins of Israelite Law," in *Essays on Old Testament History and Religion* (Oxford: Blackwell, 1966), pp. 79-132.

11. See M. Noth, *The Deuteronomistic History* (Sheffield: JSOT, 1981).

12. See T. Fretheim, *Deuteronomic History* (Nashville: Abingdon, 1983), pp. 29-34, for a list of such criteria.

13. For details, see J. Blenkinsopp, *The Pentateuch,* pp. 47-50.

14. M. Noth, *The History of Israel,* rev. ed. (New York: Harper & Row, 1960); J. Bright, *A History of Israel,* 3rd ed. (Philadelphia: Westminster,

1982); cf. also J. Hayes and J. Maxwell Miller, *Israelite and Judean History* (Philadelphia: Westminster, 1977).

15. For a survey of more recent historiographical efforts, see J. Blenkinsopp, *The Pentateuch*, pp. 37-42, 174-78; see also P. Davies, *In Search of "Ancient Israel"* (Sheffield: JSOT, 1992).

16. Representative studies include R. Alter, *The Art of Biblical Narrative* (New York: Basic, 1981); A. Berlin, *Poetics and Interpretation of Biblical Narratives* (Sheffield: Almond, 1983); D. Gunn and D. Fewell, *Narrative in the Hebrew Bible* (Oxford: Oxford University Press, 1993); M. Sternberg, *The Poetics of Biblical Narrative* (Bloomington: Indiana University Press, 1985).

17. See T. Mann, *The Book of the Torah: The Narrative Integrity of the Pentateuch* (Atlanta: John Knox, 1988); D. Clines, *The Theme of the Pentateuch* (Sheffield: JSOT, 1978). Other important studies of portions of the Pentateuch include P. Trible, *God and the Rhetoric of Sexuality* (Philadelphia: Fortress, 1978); D. Fewell and D. Gunn, *Gender, Power, and Promise: The Subject of the Bible's First Story* (Nashville: Abingdon, 1993); S. Jeansonne, *The Women of Genesis* (Minneapolis: Fortress, 1990); and J. P. Fokkelman, *Narrative Art in Genesis* (Assen, Netherlands: van Gorcum, 1975).

18. See G. Aichele et al., *The Postmodern Bible* (New Haven, CT: Yale University Press, 1995), pp. 20-69, and the bibliography noted there.

19. For some recent essays that use and assess this and related approaches, see A. Brenner, ed., *A Feminist Companion to Genesis* (Sheffield: Sheffield Academic Press, 1993); A. Brenner, *A Feminist Companion to Exodus to Deuteronomy* (Sheffield: Sheffield Academic Press, 1994); M. Tolbert and F. Segovia, eds., *Reading from this Place: Social Location and Biblical Interpretation*, vol. 1 (Minneapolis: Fortress, 1995); J. C. Exum and D. Clines, eds., *The New Literary Criticism and the Hebrew Bible* (Sheffield: JSOT, 1993); B. Stratton, *Out of Eden: Reading, Rhetoric, and Ideology in Genesis 2–3* (Sheffield: JSOT, 1995).

20. For reflections on the task of discerning the theology *in* the text, see T. Fretheim, *Exodus* (Louisville: John Knox, 1991), pp. 10-12. See also the somewhat different approach of D. Gowan, *Theology in Exodus: Biblical Theology in the Form of a Commentary* (Louisville: Westminster/John Knox, 1994), pp. ix-xviii.

21. R. Rendtorff, *Canon and Theology: Overtures to an Old Testament Theology* (Minneapolis: Fortress, 1993), pp. 40-41.

2. A PROPOSAL FOR READING THE PENTATEUCH

1. See T. Fretheim, "The Reclamation of Creation: Redemption and Law in Exodus" *Interpretation* 45 (1991): 354-65; "Creator, Creature, and Co-creation in Genesis 1–2," in *All Things New: Essays in Honor of Roy A. Harrisville*, Word and World Supplement 1 (1992), pp. 11-20.

2. See H. W. Wolff, "The Kerygma of the Yahwist," *Interpretation* 20 (1966), 131-58.

3. See T. Fretheim, *Exodus* (Louisville: John Knox, 1991), pp. 303-5.

4. See C. Westermann, *Blessing in the Bible and the Life of the Church,* trans. K. Crim (Philadelphia: Fortress, 1978).

5. See F. Kermode, *The Sense of an Ending* (Oxford: Oxford University Press, 1966).

6. An exception for Deuteronomy is D. Olson, *Deuteronomy and the Death of Moses: A Theological Reading* (Minneapolis: Fortress, 1994).

7. See T. Mann, *The Book of the Torah: The Narrative Integrity of the Pentateuch* (Atlanta: John Knox, 1988), p. 161.

8. See J. Blenkinsopp, *The Pentateuch* (New York: Doubleday, 1992), p. 51.

9. T. Mann, *The Book of the Torah,* p. 159.

10. See D. Freedman, "Pentateuch," in *Interpreter's Dictionary of the Bible,* III (Nashville: Abingdon, 1962), pp. 712-14.

11. See T. Dozeman, *God on the Mountain* (Atlanta: Scholars Press, 1990).

12. See T. Fretheim, "The Book of Genesis," *New Interpreter's Bible,* vol. 1 (Nashville: Abingdon, 1994), pp. 580-81.

3. THE BOOK OF GENESIS

1. See R. Cohn, "Narrative Structure and Canonical Perspective in Genesis," *JSOT* 25 (1983), 3-16.

2. For traditional matters of introduction, see C. Westermann, *Genesis 1–11: A Commentary* (Minneapolis: Augsburg, 1984), pp. 1-73. For newer approaches, see B. Stratton, *Out of Eden: Reading, Rhetoric, and Ideology in Genesis 2–3* (Sheffield: JSOT, 1995). See also W. Brueggemann, *Genesis* (Atlanta: John Knox, 1982); G. von Rad, *Genesis* (Philadelphia: Westminster, 1972).

3. See J. Rogerson, *Genesis 1 11* (Sheffield: JSOT, 1991), pp. 41-55.

4. See G. Rendsburg, *The Redaction of Genesis* (Winona Lake, IN: Eisenbrauns, 1986).

5. See T. Fretheim, "The Book of Genesis," in *The New Interpreter's Bible,* vol. 1 (Nashville: Abingdon, 1994), p. 356.

6. See P. Trible, *God and the Rhetoric of Sexuality* (Philadelphia: Fortress, 1978), pp. 79-81.

7. See H. White, *Narration and Discourse in the Book of Genesis* (Cambridge: Cambridge University Press, 1991), pp. 133-37.

8. See P. Trible, *God and the Rhetoric of Sexuality,* pp. 123-32.

9. See C. Westermann, *Genesis 12–36: A Continental Commentary* (Minneapolis: Augsburg, 1985); and *Genesis 37–50: A Continental Commentary* (Minneapolis: Augsburg, 1986).

10. See G. Rendsburg, *The Redaction of Genesis,* pp. 27-52.

11. See W. L. Humphreys, *Joseph and His Family: A Literary Study* (Columbia: University of South Carolina Press, 1988).

12. S. Jeansonne, *The Women of Genesis* (Minneapolis: Fortress, 1990).

13. See D. Clines, *The Theme of the Pentateuch* (Sheffield: JSOT, 1978).

14. See T. Fretheim, "The Book of Genesis," pp. 494-501.

4. THE BOOK OF EXODUS

1. For detail, see T. Fretheim, *Exodus* (Louisville: John Knox, 1991); T. Fretheim, "Because the Whole Earth Is Mine: Narrative and Theme in Exodus," *Interpretation*, 50 (1996).

2. See T. Fretheim, *Exodus*, p. 100.

3. See J. Durham, *Exodus* (Waco, TX: Word, 1987); D. Gowan, *Theology in Exodus: Biblical Theology in the Form of a Commentary* (Louisville: Westminster/John Knox, 1994), pp. 175-76.

4. See T. Fretheim, *Exodus*, pp. 133-36.

5. W. Brueggemann, "The Book of Exodus," in *The New Interpreter's Bible*, vol. 1. (Nashville: Abingdon, 1994), p. 834.

6. See B. Childs, *The Book of Exodus* (Philadelphia: Westminster, 1974), p. 367.

7. See H. W. Wolff, "The Kerygma of the Yahwist," *Interpretation* 20 (1966), pp. 131-58.

8. See J. Levenson, *Creation and the Persistence of Evil: The Jewish Drama of Divine Omnipotence* (San Francisco: Harper & Row, 1988), p. 86.

5. THE BOOK OF LEVITICUS

1. For these distinctions, see T. Fretheim, "Salvation in the Bible vs. Salvation in the Church," *Word and World* 13 (1993): 363-72.

2. See J. Milgrom, *Leviticus 1–16*, Anchor Bible, vol. 3 (New York: Doubleday, 1991).

3. See R. Nelson, *Raising Up a Faithful Priest: Community and Priesthood in Biblical Theology* (Minneapolis: Fortress, 1993).

4. For a fuller explication, see T. Fretheim, *Exodus* (Louisville: John Knox, 1991), pp. 201-7.

5. See T. Fretheim, "The Reclamation of Creation," *Interpretation* 45 (1991), 362-65.

6. See T. Fretheim, *Exodus*, pp. 268-72, for the long-noted ties between tabernacle and creation.

7. F. Gorman, *The Ideology of Ritual: Space, Time and Status in the Priestly Theology* (Sheffield: JSOT, 1990), p. 230.

8. H. H. Rowley, *Worship in Ancient Israel* (London: SPCK, 1967), p. 140.

9. G. von Rad, *Old Testament Theology*, I (New York: Harper & Row, 1962), p. 262.

10. See R. Nelson, *Raising Up a Faithful Priest*, pp. 17-38.

11. Mary Douglas, *Purity and Danger: An Analysis of the Concepts of Pollution and Taboo* (London: Routledge & Kegan Paul, 1966).

6. THE BOOK OF NUMBERS

1. See J. Milgrom, *The JPS Torah Commentary: Numbers* (Philadelphia: Jewish Publication Society, 1990), pp. xvii-xxi. See also G. Wenham, *Numbers: An Introduction and Commentary* (Downers Grove, IL: Inter-

Varsity, 1981); T. R. Ashley, *The Book of Numbers* (Grand Rapids: Eerdmans, 1993); B. A. Levine, *Numbers 1–20,* Anchor Bible, vol. 5 (New York: Doubleday, 1993).

2. See D. Olson, *The Death of the Old and the Birth of the New* (Chico, CA: Scholars Press, 1985).

3. See D. Clines, *The Theme of the Pentateuch* (Sheffield: JSOT, 1978), pp. 53-57.

4. See T. Fretheim, *Exodus* (Louisville: John Knox, 1991), pp. 175-76.

5. On Moses' prayers in Numbers, see S. Balentine, *Prayer in the Hebrew Bible: The Drama of the Divine-Human Dialogue* (Minneapolis: Fortress, 1993), pp. 123-45.

6. See R. Nelson, *Raising Up a Faithful Priest: Community and Priesthood in Biblical Theology* (Minneapolis: Fortress, 1993), pp. 1-15.

7. See T. Fretheim, *The Suffering of God: An Old Testament Perspective* (Minneapolis· Fortress, 1984), pp. 107-26.

7. THE BOOK OF DEUTERONOMY

1. See P. Miller, *Deuteronomy* (Louisville: John Knox, 1990) pp. 10-15.

2. D. Olson, *Deuteronomy and the Death of Moses: A Theological Reading* (Minneapolis: Fortress, 1994), pp. 49-61.

3. Ibid., pp. 62-125.

4. Ibid., p. 128.

5. Ibid., p. 6.

6. On land in Deuteronomy, see P. Miller, *Deuteronomy,* pp. 44-52.

7. See D. Clines, *The Theme of the Pentateuch* (Sheffield: JSOT, 1978), p. 59.

8. See T. Fretheim, "The Reclamation of Creation," *Interpretation* 45 (1991), and the bibliography given there.

9. See P. Miller, *Deuteronomy,* pp. 39-42; T. Fretheim, *Deuteronomic History* (Nashville. Abingdon, 1983), pp. 68-75.

10. See G. von Rad, *Deuteronomy* (Philadelphia: Westminster, 1966), p. 13.

SELECTED BIBLIOGRAPHY

Alter, Robert. *The Art of Biblical Narrative.* New York: Basic, 1981.

Ashley, Timothy. *The Book of Numbers.* Grand Rapids: Eerdmans, 1993.

Balentine, Samuel. *Prayer in the Hebrew Bible: The Drama of the Divine Human Dialogue.* Minneapolis: Fortress, 1993.

Barton, John. *Reading the Old Testament: Method in Biblical Study.* Philadelphia: Westminster, 1984.

Berlin, Adele. *Poetics and Interpretation of Biblical Narratives.* Sheffield: Almond, 1983.

Blenkinsopp, Joseph. *The Pentateuch: An Introduction to the First Five Books of the Bible.* New York: Doubleday, 1992.

Brenner, Althalya, ed. *A Feminist Companion to Genesis.* Sheffield: Sheffield Academic Press, 1993.

————. *A Feminist Companion to Exodus to Deuteronomy.* Sheffield: Sheffield Academic Press, 1994.

Brueggemann, Walter. *Genesis.* Atlanta: John Knox, 1982.

————. "The Book of Exodus." In *The New Interpreter's Bible*, vol. 1. Nashville: Abingdon, 1994.

Brueggemann, Walter and H. W. Wolff. *The Vitality of Old Testament Traditions.* 2nd ed. Atlanta: John Knox, 1982.

Childs, Brevard. *The Book of Exodus.* Philadelphia: Westminster, 1974.

————. *Introduction to the Old Testament as Scripture.* Philadelphia: Fortress, 1979.

Clines, David. *The Theme of the Pentateuch.* Sheffield: JSOT, 1978.

Coats, George W. *Rebellion in the Wilderness.* Nashville: Abingdon, 1968.

Damrosch, David. *The Narrative Covenant*. San Francisco: Harper & Row, 1987.

Douglas, Mary. *Purity and Danger: An Analysis of the Concepts of Pollution and Taboo*. London: Routledge & Kegan Paul, 1966.

Dozeman, Thomas. *God on the Mountain*. Atlanta: Scholars Press, 1990.

Durham, John. *Exodus*. Waco, TX: Word, 1987.

Exum, J. Cheryl, and David Clines, eds. *The New Literary Criticism and the Hebrew Bible*. Sheffield: JSOT, 1993.

Fewell, Danna, and David Gunn. *Gender, Power, and Promise: The Subject of the Bible's First Story*. Nashville: Abingdon, 1993.

Fokkelman, J. P. *Narrative Art in Genesis*. Assen, Netherlands: van Gorcum, 1975.

Fretheim, Terence. *Exodus*. Louisville: John Knox, 1991.

———. "The Book of Genesis." *The New Interpreter's Bible*, vol. 1. Nashville: Abingdon, 1994.

———. *The Suffering of God: An Old Testament Perspective*. Philadelphia: Fortress, 1984.

Friedman, Richard. "Torah (Pentateuch)," Anchor Bible Dictionary, vol. 6. New York: Doubleday, 1992.

Gorman, Frank. *The Ideology of Ritual. Space, Time, and Status in the Priestly Theology*. Sheffield: JSOT, 1990.

Gowan, Donald. *From Eden to Babel: A Commentary on the Book of Genesis 1–11*. Grand Rapids: Eerdmans, 1988.

———. *Theology in Exodus: Biblical Theology in the Form of a Commentary*. Louisville: Westminster/John Knox, 1994.

Gunn, David, and Danna Fewell. *Narrative in the Hebrew Bible*. Oxford: Oxford University Press, 1993.

Hamilton, Victor. *The Book of Genesis, Chapters 1–17*. Grand Rapids: Eerdmans, 1990.

Humphreys, W. Lee. *Joseph and His Family: A Literary Study*. Columbia: University of South Carolina Press, 1988.

Janzen, J. G. *Genesis 12–50: Abraham and All the Families of the Earth*. Grand Rapids: Eerdmans, 1993.

Jeansonne, Sharon. *The Women of Genesis*. Minneapolis: Fortress, 1990.

Jenson, P. *Graded Holiness: A Key to the Priestly Conception of the World*. Sheffield: JSOT, 1992.

Kaiser, Walter, "The Book of Leviticus." In *The New Interpreter's Bible*, vol. 1. Nashville: Abingdon, 1994.

Levenson, Jon. *Sinai and Zion: An Entry into the Jewish Bible.* San Francisco: Harper & Row, 1987.

———. *Creation and the Persistence of Evil: The Jewish Drama of Divine Omnipotence.* San Francisco: Harper & Row, 1988.

Levine, Baruch. *Numbers 1–20.* Anchor Bible, vol. 5. New York: Doubleday, 1993.

———. *Leviticus.* JPS Torah Commentary. Philadelphia: Jewish Publication Society, 1989.

Lohfink, Norbert. *Theology of the Pentateuch: Themes of the Priestly Narrative and Deuteronomy.* Minneapolis: Fortress, 1994.

Mann, Thomas. *The Book of the Torah: The Narrative Integrity of the Pentateuch.* Atlanta: John Knox, 1988.

Milgrom, Jacob. *Leviticus 1–16.* Anchor Bible, vol. 3. New York: Doubleday, 1991.

———. *Numbers.* JPS Torah Commentary. Philadelphia: Jewish Publication Society, 1990.

Miller, Patrick. *Deuteronomy.* Louisville: John Knox, 1990.

Moberly, R. W. L. *The Old Testament of the Testament: Patriarchal Narratives and Mosaic Yahwism.* Minneapolis: Fortress, 1992.

Nelson, Richard. *Raising Up a Faithful Priest: Community and Priesthood in Biblical Theology.* Minneapolis: Fortress, 1993.

Newsom, Carol and Sharon Ringe, eds. *The Women's Bible Commentary.* Louisville: Westminster/John Knox, 1992.

Nicholson, Ernest. *God and His People: Covenant and Theology in the Old Testament.* Oxford: Clarendon, 1986.

Noth, Martin. *A History of Pentateuchal Traditions.* Englewood Cliffs, NJ: Prentice-Hall, 1972.

Olson, Dennis. *Deuteronomy and the Death of Moses: A Theological Reading.* Minneapolis: Fortress, 1994.

———. *The Death of the Old and the Birth of the New: The Framework of the Book of Numbers and the Pentateuch.* Chico, CA: Scholars Press, 1985.

Patrick, Dale. *Old Testament Law.* Atlanta: John Knox, 1984.

Ramsey, George. *The Quest for the Historical Israel.* Atlanta: John Knox, 1981.

Rendsburg, Gary. *The Redaction of Genesis.* Winona Lake, IN: Eisenbrauns, 1986.

Rendtorff, Rolf. *The Old Testament: An Introduction.* Philadelphia: Fortress, 1986.

———. *The Problem of the Process of Transmission in the Pentateuch.* Sheffield: JSOT, 1990.

Rogerson, John. *Genesis 1–11.* Sheffield: JSOT, 1991.

Sailhamer, John. *The Pentateuch as Narrative: A Biblical-Theological Commentary.* Grand Rapids: Zondervan, 1992.

Sarna, Nahum. *Exodus.* JPS Torah Commentary. Philadelphia: Jewish Publication Society, 1991.

———. *Genesis.* JPS Torah Commentary. Philadelphia: Jewish Publication Society, 1989.

Sternberg, Meir. *The Poetics of Biblical Narrative.* Bloomington: Indiana University Press, 1985.

Stratton, Beverly. *Out of Eden: Reading, Rhetoric and Ideology in Genesis 2–3.* Sheffield: JSOT, 1996.

Tate, W. Randolph. *Biblical Interpretation: An Integrated Approach.* Peabody, MA: Hendrickson, 1991.

Trible, Phyllis. *God and the Rhetoric of Sexuality.* Philadelphia: Fortress, 1978.

von Rad, Gerhard. *Deuteronomy.* Philadelphia: Westminster, 1966.

———. "The Form-Critical Problem of the Hexateuch." In *The Problem of the Hexateuch and Other Essays.* New York: McGraw-Hill; Edinburgh: Oliver & Boyd, 1966.

———. *Genesis.* Philadelphia: Westminster, 1972.

———. *Old Testament Theology,* I. New York: Harper & Row, 1962.

Weinfeld, Moshe. *Deuteronomy 1–11.* Anchor Bible, vol. 5. New York: Doubleday, 1991.

Wenham, Gordon. *The Book of Leviticus.* Grand Rapids: Eerdmans, 1979.

———. *Genesis 1–15.* Waco, TX: Word, 1987.

———. *Numbers: An Introduction and Commentary.* Downer's Grove, IL.: Inter-Varsity, 1981.

Westermann, Claus. *Blessing in the Bible and the Life of the Church.* Translated by K. Crim. Philadelphia: Fortress, 1978.

———. *Genesis 1–11: A Continental Commentary.* Minneapolis: Augsburg, 1984.

———. *Genesis 12–36: A Continental Commentary.* Minneapolis: Augsburg, 1985.

———. *Genesis 37–50: A Continental Commentary.* Minneapolis: Augsburg, 1986.

White, Hugh. *Narration and Discourse in the Book of Genesis.* Cambridge: Cambridge University Press, 1991.

Whybray, R. N. *Introduction to the Pentateuch*. Grand Rapids: Eerdmans, 1995.

———. *The Making of the Pentateuch: A Methodological Study.* Sheffield: JSOT, 1987.

INDEX

181